# EARTH ENERGIES

The Theosophical Publishing House
P.O. Box 270
Wheaton, IL 60189-0270

A publication of the Theosophical Publishing House,
a department of the Theosophical Society in America.


**Library of Congress Cataloging-in-Publication Data**

King, Serge.
  Earth energies : a quest for the hidden power of the planet / Serge
Kahili King.
    p.  cm.
  Includes index.
  ISBN 0-8356-0682-1 (pbk.) : $12.00
  1. Vril.    I. Title.
BF1623.V7K56   1992
133 — dc20                      92-50146
                                   CIP


9 8 7 6 5 4 3 2   *      95 96 97 98 99


This edition is printed on acid-free paper that meets the
American National Standards Institute Z39.48 Standard

Printed in the United States of America by Versa Press

# EARTH ENERGIES

*A*
*QUEST for*
*the HIDDEN POWER*
*of the PLANET*

## SERGE KAHILI KING

*This publication made possible with*
*the assistance of the Kern Foundation*

QUEST BOOKS
The Theosophical Publishing House
Wheaton, Illinois, U.S.A.; Adyar, Madras, India

To all those in the past who have—and all those in the future who will—"Let that which is unknown become known," and to the hundreds of volunteers who helped me in my research. My heartfelt thanks also to Susan Pa'iniu Floyd and Ken Ka'imi Stokes for their considerable assistance in preparing the manuscript.

# Contents

# Preface

We are of the earth, earthy. We certainly have a mind
and/or spirit which can transcend this planet both
physically and metaphysically, but in addition we have
animal bodies with animal natures which respond to
and interact with the natural forces of the Earth. You
are familiar with some of these forces such as electricity, magnetism, and gravity. Modern science recognizes
two others you may be less familiar with, which are
called the strong and weak nuclear forces. Shamans,
mystics, metaphysicians and more liberal scientists
recognize additional forces that can be termed "psychoenergetic," a Russian term meaning that they interact
with the mind as well as the body. These are the ones
discussed in this book, because they are so little
known, so influential in our lives and so very useful.
Dr. William Tiller, professor of materials science at
Stanford University, has said in regard to experiments
with these forces, "We seem to be dealing with *new
energy fields* completely different from those known to
us via conventional science." However, they are new
only to conventional scientists.

My own background includes extensive training from
the age of fourteen in social and physical sciences as

well as metaphysics. Shamanism, a healing path with an ancient tradition of combining the energies of the mind and the Earth, is my particular framework. But it was through my studies in science and metaphysics that I came to realize the amazing connections between the experiences and researches of a vast number of people experimenting in the field of psychoenergetics.

Preparations for a career in archeology led me to massive evidence of unusual energy use in the ancient past. A degree in Asian Studies opened me to the psychoenergetic ideas of Japan, China and India. Degrees, work and travel related to international management helped me to discover psychoenergetics in Latin America and Africa. My studies in psychology introduced me to the psychoenergetic researches of Mesmer, Reichenbach and Reich. And metaphysical research revealed the psychoenergetic effects of pyramids, radionics and a host of other phenomena. All of this, of course, was developed on the foundation of my basic shamanic perspective, which emphasizes the practical application of mental and environmental energies for the good of the community.

I tested many of the ideas in this book through experiments conducted under the aegis of Aloha International, a nonprofit organization dedicated to the betterment of life on Earth. Some of those experiments are mentioned in these pages. The hundreds of volunteers used as subjects came from members, students and even people off the street. The procedures we employed, based on a scientific format, are outlined in the Appendix, so you can apply them to your own experiments if you wish.

This area of research deals with the energies behind extraordinary phenomena like nonphysical healing, levitation, telekinesis, superstrength and many others in which the mind is always an important factor. Al-

though we call the phenomena extraordinary because
they do not fit the standard model of the way things
are supposed to work, they are by no means uncommon. Every culture in the world has an abundance of
stories about them and experiences of them. Further on
I present evidence which suggests that the basic
knowledge of this field is incredibly old. Nevertheless
what is happening today is new because it is a syn-
thesis, a product of our times. This is a period of
*rediscovery,* a renaissance, with strong parallels to the
Renaissance that took place in Europe. My quest in this
book consists of examining a variety of sources relating
to psychoenergetics, making valid correlations between
them and describing experiments based on them whenever possible. The aim is to come up with a set of
observations about the energy or energies involved that
can be of practical value for immediate use and for
future research.

You are about to enter a study in which familiar
classification systems have a strong tendency to break
down completely, an area where science, religion,
technology and magic lose their sharp definitions,
overlap and blend strangely with one another. Right
now a quiet revolution is going on throughout the
world. Tradition-fettered people are refusing to glance
at this work or are scoffing at it. At the same time a
large number of scientists, engineers and laypeople
in many nations are carefully and for the most part
silently moving into realms of knowledge that can make
our existing technology so outdated that the society of
the twentieth century will seem the equivalent of the
Stone Age. The revolution is taking place in laboratories that are shiny, modern and well equipped, as
well as in converted garages and makeshift corners of
homes. This exciting and mysterious leap into the
unknown will affect every human being on earth.

To quote again from Tiller regarding this search for unknown energies, "We are likely to find that there is only *one* energy which has manifold expressions depending on the state of consciousness which interacts with the energy." There is no commonly accepted name for this one energy because most investigators work independently, and many have honestly thought they were the first to discover the effects they produced. John White and Stanley Krippner, editors of *Future Science,* listed one hundred separate names for it from ancient and modern times. Therefore, in order to avoid repeating "this energy" all the time, I will arbitrarily use the word *vril.* According to Louis Pauwels and Jacques Bergier, authors of *The Morning of the Magicians,* the concept of *vril* was first mentioned by the French writer Jacolliot in the eighteenth century and later used in a nineteenth-century novel by Bulwer Lytton. It refers to a form of energy somewhat like "the Force" described in the *Star Wars* movies that, in Lytton's story, was mastered by a race living in the center of the earth. Thus *vril* will serve our purpose well as a generic term for an energy related both to the mind and to Nature.

Evidence for the hypothesis of one energy behind all the phenomena is suggested by the fact that the same phenomena can be produced from apparently diverse sources of energy. I call this the "Law of the Elephant." If it looks like an elephant, walks like an elephant, smells like an elephant and talks like an elephant, it's probably an elephant. For instance, magnetism, electricity, crystals, sunlight, geometric forms, human hands and human thought all display quite different energetic effects, yet in certain areas, such as plant growth and healing, they all show identical energetic effects. The hypothesis to be explored is that, in addition to their unique aspects, many sources also have a single energy in common, in the same way that the different physical elements all have electrons in common.

The purpose of this book, then, is fourfold: 1) to expand your ideas about energy and its relation to the mind; 2) to suggest evidence for a single "protoenergy" which is either a carrier for or an effect of all other energies; 3) to give you practical ways to use the ideas presented; and 4) to stimulate further research. Join me in exploring *vril*, the unseen energy that affects our minds, bodies, and environment.

# 1
# Clues from the Ancients

Myth, legend, history and archeology are full of clues that the ancients used *vril* in various ways. There is evidence that it was understood widely in many long-gone cultures. While we can only speculate on the ancients' psychoenergetic ideas and practices, later chapters present more recent practices closer to home that corroborate the existence and influence of this powerful unseen energy. Meanwhile, in discussing psychoenergetics of the past, I also share some personal experiences.

## Traditions of India

From Indian philosophy, we get the concept of three kinds of force or energy: *prana*, *akasa* and *kundalini*. Different schools disagree somewhat on exactly what they are. In general, *prana* is considered a free form of energy in the atmosphere and also the vitalizing energy in living things. It is taken into the body through food and by breathing. By the use of certain techniques an abnormal amount can be ingested and stored in the body and used to improve health, as well as to be directed mentally to help others and to perform such

**1**

feats as levitation. *Kundalini* is described as a force stored at the base of the spine which can be induced to rise up the spine to the top of the head and in so doing is said to open chakras or psychic centers and lead either to enlightenment or to physical and psychic damage. Some claim raising *kundalini* is the only way to enlightenment, but some warn that it should not be attempted unless one is in the extended care of a "master"; otherwise one could literally burn oneself up as the energy tears its way upward. *Akasa* (or *akashia, akasha*) is more mysterious than the other two, being variously described as an energy and as an etheric fluid. I return to this concept several times in the book.

Virtually everything written about *prana* and *kundalini* comes from yogis, occultists and similar writers. Hardly anything has been written from a purely objective point of view, simply describing effects so that one can understand them.

## Out of the Far East

The scientific achievements of ancient China were far ahead of any other civilization of the time except, perhaps, Egypt. Chinese alchemists were trying to change base metals to gold, to discover the secret of immortality and to reach perfection in body, mind and spirit long before the birth of Christ. Their methods and terminology were remarkably similar to those of European alchemists during the Middle Ages.

One Chinese accomplishment was the manufacture of aluminum bronze. Objects of that material have been found dating back to the second century A.D. As far as we know now, the only way to make such an alloy is by electrolysis, so either they knew of that process or used another, unknown to us as yet. Magnetism was known in the same era and was used for orientation by 2 A.D.

More remarkably, a seismograph was invented between 78 and 139 A.D. that, in the words of Louis Pauwels and Jacques Bergier, "implies the application of advanced scientific principles and postulates a knowledge of the earth's structure, of mathematics and even of the propagation of waves, the origin of which is unknown." Such knowledge would have taken centuries to build up by the means we use today.

In Chinese writings of the first millennium B.C. there are many references to "magic mirrors." Some sources state that they were used to capture spirits, though this is not readily accepted today. According to Pauwels and Bergier, they "have extremely complicated high reliefs on the back of the looking glass. When direct sunlight falls on the mirror, the high reliefs, which are separated from the surface by a reflecting glass, become visible. This does not happen in artificial light. The phenomenon is scientifically inexplicable." It is also said that when set up in pairs they transmit images to form a kind of television. Going further back into Chinese legendary history, we find evidence of airplanes, spaceships, terrible weapons of destruction, marvelous healing abilities and men who have mastered the technique of flying.

All technological exploits require energy. What kind of energy concepts do we find among the Chinese? There are two, which turn out to be quite similar to the Hindu ideas of *prana* and *kundalini.* First there is *li,* which means strength, energy or force. The term, with qualifying additions, can be applied to anything from electricity to gravity to mind-force. According to esoteric literature, *li* alone is used when referring to the energy behind levitation and other supernormal phenomena. In its written form the Chinese language is

descended from pictographs, somewhat like hieroglyphics, and individual ideas are formed into what are
called "characters." Most characters are composed of
two or more basic characters and relatively few are
single. The character for *li* is a single type, indicating
that it is an extremely ancient concept.

The other type of energy, called *ch'i,* is associated
mostly with the body. Its root meaning is "breath."
According to theory, its operation forms the basis for
acupuncture. *Ch'i* is said to circulate through the body
in channels called "meridians." When these meridians
get blocked, there is too much *ch'i* in one part of the
body and too little in another. Thus, says the theory,
disease and pain develop. The purpose of acupuncture
is to balance the flow and restore harmony in the body.
There is no doubt that acupuncture works, although
modern medicine has no explanation for it within the
framework of Western tradition. *Ch'i* is also prominent
in the practice of *t'ai ch'i ch'uan* and *ch'i kung,* whose
purpose is to cause the *ch'i* to flow easily throughout
the body, as well as in Chinese martial arts where it is
concentrated in the extremities for fighting. There are
numerous tales from China, often dramatized in modern movies, of martial arts masters using the power of
*ch'i* for such superhuman feats as lifting, breaking,
leaping and flying, not to mention dispatching hordes
of opponents. Western martial artists tend to discount
the *ch'i* aspects of Chinese tradition and to focus only
on the physical skills.

I have practiced *t'ai ch'i ch'uan* and *ch'i kung* and
have felt the *ch'i* or *vril* flow through my body. And I
have experienced powerful effects from the practice of
martial arts. The famous martial artist Bruce Lee had a
technique he called the "one-inch punch" whereby the
mental focus of *ch'i* in his fist enabled him to knock a
man across a room with a punch that traveled no far-
ther than one inch. Intrigued by this, I practiced until

I could knock one of my pillow-protected sons back several feet with the one-inch punch. When I was in the Marine Corps I lost my temper once and hit a man on the chin, automatically focusing my energy as I did so. He flew off the ground and back five feet before landing. Amazingly, I never actually felt any contact with his chin, and he did not have the slightest bruise.

The Japanese concept of *ki* is virtually identical to *ch'i*. Japan also has the ancient tradition of the recently popularized *ninja,* who were supposedly able to use their *ki* for superhuman feats and magical abilities. One of their presumed powers was the ability to become invisible. Using techniques of breathing and mental focus I have used this on a number of occasions, although it appears to work by diverting the attention of others rather than causing any physical change. To share another Marine Corps story, it was the policy when I was in, for every Marine, at least in the infantry, to spend thirty days a year on kitchen duty. So every month the troops lined up and the men to go on "K.P." were selected. I felt that I could serve my country better in the field than in the kitchen, so when the troops lined up for selection I just "turned invisible." Strange as it may sound, the fact is that I served three years without any kitchen duty.

## Middle Eastern Mysteries

At Baalbek in Lebanon there are enormous stone blocks, quarried, shaped and carried to a temple site by means unknown, not only to the ancients as far as we know, but by means unknown to our present technology. Three of the blocks at the temple site weigh one thousand tons each. There is not a crane in the world that could lift them, even supposing there were a vehicle that could carry them. And one dressed block still at the quarry site weighs two thousand tons, im-

possible to move by our present standards, but the
stones are uncomfortably there. Other sites containing
gigantic blocks abound in the Middle East and around
the Mediterranean. Egypt contains some of the best
known examples. Not only the pyramids, but massive
temple foundations and colossal statues demonstrate an
unknown technique of transportation. Of course, a
number of plausible theories about the construction of
the pyramids exist.

In ancient Egypt legend tells of rods of power that
could be charged by the mind or energy of priests.
They could then be pointed at massive blocks of stone,
such as found in the Great Pyramid, causing them to
rise in the air and move a few feet before falling.
According to legend the stones in the pyramids, in
massive temple foundations and in colossal statues
were moved in this way to the construction site and
into place. Since we have no explanation that satisfies
everyone of how these huge stones were moved, we
might explore the use of rods of power in ancient
Egypt. Their art and literature provide ample evidence
that Egyptians used rods of different kinds.

The *ankh* or *crux ansata* is a kind of cross with a
circle at the top, like the astronomical symbol for
Venus. It is found frequently in the hieroglyphics and
has been translated as meaning "life." It has long been
considered a symbol for occult wisdom, and with the
rise in popularity of that field, the ankh has been made
into a rather faddish piece of jewelry. But a careful
look at Egyptian frescoes and sculpture shows that it
was not always worn. Instead it was often large enough
to hold in the hand, quite in the manner of a weapon
or tool, either with the fingers curled through the circle
or with the straight end gripped in the fist. Some
legends state that it emitted a bolt of lightning that
could destroy one's enemies, and some frescoes seem
to show this or something similar happening. Others

seem to indicate that it was used in a healing manner.

How was the ankh made and of what materials? On a visit to the Cairo Museum in 1980 I made extensive observations of the oldest ankhs on display. Some were made of mixed materials, either different metals or combinations of metal and wood, and the crossbar was made in the form of a knot tying the circle and shaft together. This is pure speculation, but this construction may be related to positive and negative polarities of energy represented by the obvious male and female symbolism.

Then there are curious rods, four to five inches long, frequently shown in the hands of statues representing gods, kings, queens, princes and overseers. The latter generally hold only one rod, while the others almost always are shown holding two, one in each hand. Egyptologists have no clue as to what they were for. The rods are too small to be symbols of power because they would not be noticeable from a few yards away, and the markings, size and shape are not appropriate for royal seals. For a possible explanation we can turn once again to esoteric tradition. Information received from various mediums over the years indicates that the purpose of the rods was to increase the power of one's body energy field to the point where the energy could be directed at will for both psychic and physical objectives. The small rods were supposedly made of different materials designed to generate a current flow between them. One combination claimed was carbon and magnetic iron, another was copper or bronze and tin. Some were reported to be composed of tubes within tubes.

I have conducted many experiments with several hundred volunteers to demonstrate that some kind of energy flow is stimulated between these different materials, either when placed in the hand or just in close proximity to one. The flow is especially obvious when they are aligned east/west or north/south. Physiologically, subjects report a feeling of warmth, tingling, current or just well-being. Often they report feeling stimulated for several hours after holding the materials for only a few minutes. Some investigators found that galvanometric skin responses are altered after holding the materials. On the other hand, some report depleting effects that seem to depend on the orientation of the rods.

We know that Egyptian statues and paintings show figures holding mysterious rods that must have served some purpose. Psychic sources describe the materials and purpose, and an objective effect has been found when these materials are held. These facts are not proof that Egyptians used a form of energy unknown to us, but the clues are worth considering.

Yet even if the rods did have an effect of increasing the strength of the body energy field, how was that translated into a levitating force to lift rocks, if indeed the rods just described were used for that? There is a "parlor trick" that suggests an answer. If a person lays down on the floor and six others arrange themselves around him or her and try to lift him with their fingertips, it cannot be done without great difficulty. But if those six take a number of rapid, deep breaths and then try, they can lift him or her much more easily. One theory is that by rapid breathing the six have taken extra *vril* into their systems and expended it in a concentrated beam through their fingers. Since one of the powers of *vril* is said to be levitation, the ease in raising the person after deep breathing is explained. If the Egyptians were able to accumulate a large enough charge of *vril* by means of the rods or tubes, they may have been able to discharge this in a beam through another rod or tube and thus levitate a rock, at least until the charge ran out. Then there would be a delay while the priest or whoever built up another charge could cause the rock to be lifted again. In this way the rock could hop toward the site. But of course this is just theory.

In many Egyptian paintings there are mysterious staves held by some of the figures which Egyptologists have difficulty explaining. The staff has an odd top, shaped vaguely like an animal's head, a straight shaft, and a bottom that ends in two points, like a horseshoe. In one example made of wood that I saw in a case in Cairo, the bottom section had been layered over with silver leaf. It may or may not be a coincidence that silver is the best natural electrical conductor and wood is one of the best natural insulators. This combination would produce a capacitor, a device designed to store electrical energy, or maybe *vril.* In another instance I subjectively felt what seemed to be a static electric field around a case which held a chair of King Tutankhamen. The chair was made of acacia wood covered in gold leaf. We come across the capacitor effect again later.

Finally, I have to mention other frescoes, including one in the tomb of King Tut, in which wavy lines or lightning bolts are emanating directly from the palms of the main figure. This might be a symbol of authority, but it might also symbolize healing power.

It is from the Middle Eastern *magi,* meaning priests of the Medes and Persians who were supposed to have supernatural powers, that we get the word "magic."

### Enigmas in the Americas

The popular image of the early inhabitants of North America is that of a romantic but fairly primitive race of people, yet all across this land are mystifying remnants of one or more great civilizations. There are pyramids in the Midwest that are larger in volume and area than the Great Pyramid of Egypt. Broken-down

fortresses, hardly recognizable, are more numerous
than most Americans think all throughout the Missis-
sippi Valley. When the Spaniards first arrived, they
heard many stories of the Seven Cities of Cibola, not
from just one or two tribes, but practically from coast
to coast and border to border. Many lives were lost in
a search for those cities, but it is probable that the
stories had been handed down from a far earlier time.
Canadian Indian legends tell of a time when the frozen
north was a land of luxuriant forests, and there were
great cities to the south. Peter Kolosimo in *Timeless
Earth* quotes a source in which an old Indian member
of a secret society says, "Many of us went down there
and saw the shining cities and their marvels such as
the grand homes and the men who flew into the skies
to meet the Thunderbird. Then the demons returned
and there was a terrible havoc everywhere. The few of
us who had gone down there and managed to get back
declared that the cities and all the life there had all
gone. There, where once such cities stood, there is
nothing but ruins now." The explorer William Walker
wrote that the whole region between the St. John and
Gila rivers was covered with ruins of cities, full of
vitrified rock and craters caused by fires hot enough to
liquefy any rock or metal. There was, according to
legend, terrible energy available at some time in North
America's past. Today all we can see are the actual
ruins of ancient cities left by the mysterious Anasazi,
or "Ancient Ones," in such places as Mesa Verde and
Chaco Canyon. We may not think of them as cities, but
to nomadic tribes they must have been very impressive.
No one today can adequately explain why the cities
were abandoned or what happened to the people.

The concept of a special kind of energy that can
produce marvelous effects is common among traditional North American cultures. It is called *gluskap* in

Algonquin, *orenda* in Iroquois, *kachina* in Hopi and *wakan* in Dakota. Sometimes it is considered as a force, and often it is personified as a spirit.

Mexico and Central America abound in ancient legends of flying men, levitation and destructive energies. These cultures supposedly never developed the wheel or used domestic animals. Yet in the jungle of Vera Cruz lies a sixteen-ton carved head of basalt that was transported over mountains, marshes and deep gorges from a quarry over sixty miles away, and without a scratch on it. What kind of power was used to do this? There are stories that many things were accomplished with a combination of solar and magnetic energies. One source says that Montezuma presented Cortes with two gold discs that were levitation devices, which were probably melted down later. The Aztecs had an excellent system of roads throughout Mexico, but they had no horses or wheeled vehicles. Is it reasonable to suppose that these roads were built for only foot traffic?

In South America the Incas had an even better system of roads, and yet they did not have horses or wheels, either. They also had cities and fortresses on mountaintops containing stones quarried from many miles away and somehow carried over impossible terrain. On the Gate of the Sun at Tiahuanaco are strange hieroglyphs that some American scientists now believe may represent ionic motors. Now, an ionic motor is a plasma motor, and plasma has strong correlations to the energy we are studying. I delve into the subject of plasma in a later chapter.

### Energies in Africa

Throughout Africa there is an almost universal belief in magical power, even among those who follow some form of Islam or Christianity. This power is believed to manifest not only through gods, angels and spirits, but through adept human beings as well. Most often applied to sickness or healing, it is said to also be used for flying, shape-changing, teleporting and materializing. Usually the magical power is thought to be stored in or channeled through a wide variety of amulets, talismans, stones, masks and carvings, but there are also many places that exude a special energy.

During the seven years that I spent in West Africa, I had many occasions to hear about and experience the phenomena of African *vril*. Here I can mention only a couple of incidents. For example, on the border between Togo and Dahomey (now Benin) in the village of Kounadogou, I was given some magical brass rings inscribed with secret markings and infused with power by a local shaman. When I wear them I feel filled with energy, but they do not have any other effect unless I say a special prayer, according to the shaman. In Senegal I was told of a special island in the Saloum River whose sand on one shore had healing powers. I stood there in the shallow water and could feel a strong tingling in my feet and legs. Since I was not ill, however, I could not tell if there were healing effects.

Each of the many African tribes I dealt with had its own name for *vril*.

## Polynesian Powers

Many books that deal with esoteric energy tend to list *ch'i, ki, prana* and *mana* together as if they are the same thing. While the pairs do rhyme nicely, it must be stated that *mana* does not belong in the list. *Mana* is a Polynesian word that basically means divine or spiritual power and authority or influence. It is the ability to direct energy, rather than the energy itself. In Polynesia people might have great *mana* because of their genealogy, skill, deeds, wealth, character or will, but not just because they have a lot of energy. Likewise, a stone or a piece of wood could have great *mana* because of its symbolism, traditional usage, or specific energy characteristics. Using an electrical analogy, *mana* is the equilivalent of wattage or effectiveness, rather than amperage (current), voltage (pressure) or the energy itself.

In exploring the language of Hawaii to represent Polynesia, I found that there were several words for energy. There was *ui* ("to stir up, to activate") and its near equivalent, *uila* ("light activity"), used to refer to lightning and electricity. Because of its awesome effects, the lightning bolt was often a symbol for *mana* in Hawaii, which is why it was adopted by surfers. The name of the legendary hero Maui, who performed many stupendous energetic feats, is composed of the roots *ma* and *ui,* meaning "a state of energy." Then there was *ha, ea, ki,* and *ahu-ahu,* plus other terms, all of which seem to refer to the life force in various ways or to various means of increasing it. Closely associated with energy is another term, *aka.* Its characteristics correspond closely to those of the occult force termed "ectoplasm" and "astral matter," and to the Sanskrit "akasa." There are also similarities to the nineteenth century "ether" and Mesmer's "universal magnetic fluid," to be examined in the next chapter.

Polynesian legends and history abound with stories about how various heroes and masters used their version of *vril* for healing, levitation, flying, telekinesis, fire-walking, weather control and shape-changing. And there is at least one tale of clubs being charged with *vril* and thrown at enemies to jolt them with electric-like shocks.

The great stone statues of Easter Island were moved,

according to local tradition, through the air from the quarry to their present sites. Thor Hyerdahl, a Norwegian anthropologist, showed that a small statue could be moved into a standing position with levers and an earthen ramp. But he never succeeded in demonstrating how to get the statue to the site in the first place without any scratch marks and in a land that shows no sign of ever having had enough trees to use as rollers.

At a lecture I attended in Dakar, Senegal, François Mazière, a French explorer, showed a film of his expedition to Easter Island and pointed out a section of the island which he found to be totally devoid of even bacterial life, as if everything had been killed off by the radiation of an atomic bomb. And yet there was not a dangerous level of radiation at the site. Legends tell of a great battle in ancient times. Could there have been an atomic explosion, or the use of another type of force of which we know nothing?

## A Brief Look at Britain

All over England are the remnants of straight lines known as "ley lines." They connect very ancient temple sites, stone circles, hilltops and barrows. Author John Michell in *View Over Atlantis* has presented much evidence to show that they may have been magnetic lines of force over which the ancients were supposed to be able to fly in levitated chariots. Similar "sacred" lines of force have been noted in China, Polynesia and Asia. Of special interest is Michell's theory that the layered construction of barrows and hidden chambers in many megalithic sites is related to the discovery by Wilhelm Reich that layers of different materials produce a force field of *vril* (called "orgone" by Reich) with properties related to but not the same as electromagnetism. Certain effects of *vril* can be demonstrated only when the instruments or test objects are aligned with the earth's magnetic field. Here may be an important clue to the ancient secret of levitation.

The rocks of Stonehenge must be mentioned, of course, not only because of their tradition as a power spot, but because of the extraordinary effort made by the ancient builders to obtain a special kind of stone (called "bluestone") from over two hundred miles away. On viewing and studying Stonehenge and similar sites, one gets the impression that they were built by people with scientific knowledge who had only the crudest of materials to work with, like a shipwrecked engineer who creates ingenious constructions with coconuts and bamboo.

Mention must also be made of the Irish stone towers whose purpose is as mysterious as their origin, and whose surfaces are often vitrified, made glassy from a source of high heat. Theories propose that this was caused by burning firewood piled around them, but it would have to be exceptional wood to produce a fire hot enough to melt stone. The fact is that no one now knows what the heat source was.

Also in Ireland tales are still told today of the mysterious and magical *Tuatha De Danaan,* a very ancient race with exceptional powers and magical devices who preceded the Celts.

## The Persistent Legend of Atlantis

There is much geological, cultural and biological evidence to support the existence of Atlantis, but strangely no physical archeological evidence has been found in spite of long years of searching. The more interesting question concerns the level of cultural and technological achievement in Atlantis.

In his *Timaeus,* Plato described a rich civilization
that might have been the equivalent of Rome at the
height of its glory, but there is nothing in the account
to suggest a technology anywhere near our own. In
fact, the only unusual feature is the mention of
"orichalcum," a highly esteemed precious metal that
ranked above silver and gold in value and was red in
color. It was obviously not copper, since the Egyptian
priest who recounts the tale to Solon says that it does
not exist anymore, while he does mention the use of
brass, a copper alloy.

It is not from Plato that we get the stories of airplanes, rockets, advanced psychic powers and crystal
towers that emitted fantastic amounts of an unknown
energy, but from occult sources. Among the most
prominent of these is Edgar Cayce. Over a period of
some twenty years, Cayce, while in trance, gave a
remarkably consistent story of a people who com-
manded rays and "electrical forces" of various types
and "destructive forces from the prisms." Some of
these forces were used to power airplanes and to move
stone figures, among other things. The central power
supply source was a huge crystal, apparently mounted
on a tower, which transformed energy from the sun
into useful electrical and other energies. According to
Cayce, the temple containing this crystal is located
underwater near the Bahamas, oddly enough in the
zone known as the "Devil's Triangle."

Since Cayce's time, many other mediums have
described a supercivilization of Atlantis in the same
general terms. A medium I worked with described the
great crystal in considerable detail. A capstone crystal
supposedly received the solar energy and focused it
into a crystal base containing mercury, sulphuric acid
and, unfortunately, orichalcum, which is not supposed

to exist anymore. From there it was converted into useful energy and transmitted like radio waves.

The place of Atlantis in *vril* research is difficult to assess since, unlike Egypt and the Middle East, there are no artifacts to ponder and, unlike China and India, no clear cultural tales to support its existence as an energetically advanced society. So until the occult or metaphysical sources come up with some kind of practical application of their psychic revelations of Atlantean power, the legend will have to remain nothing more than an interesting reference. After all, according to Plato, even the low-technology Greeks beat the Atlanteans in battle.

## An Overview

Archeology, history, legends, myths and psychic perceptions all point to the inescapable conclusion that the ancients were much more advanced than we give them credit for being. Feats like levitation, healing and destruction are too widespread and described in too much consistent detail for us to dismiss them lightly as fantasy. To be sure, much of what was described can be attributed to a knowledge of electricity and perhaps even lasers and atomic weapons. This is fantastic enough in itself, but we are not here to gape and wonder. What interests us are the residual details that indicate the use of a force which is not in common knowledge today.

No one source constitutes sufficient proof that there really was such a force in use. Archeology alone merely presents us with inexplicable artifacts, but that does not mean we may not find a simple explanation for them someday. We know that history can be distorted to suit the purposes of the historian. Legends and myths can be explained away as symbolism or wish-fulfillment, and psychic perception is too subject to charlatanry and distortion to be of any value by itself. It is only when we put all of these together from sources all over the world that we begin to be impressed with the heavy weight of circumstantial evidence. What we have from the ancients, then, are tantalizing clues.

In the pages to follow we start on the road to hard facts, supported by witnesses and serious experimentation. Do not expect to find hard answers, however, for all our answers lead to more questions. The hope is that you readers will be stimulated to answer some of those questions for the rest of us. The end of the quest still lies in the future, which may not be too far away.

# 2
# The Vril of Mesmer

Franz Anton Mesmer was born on May 23, 1734, and died in 1815 at the age of eighty-one. He has achieved immortality because his name is associated with a phenomenon which was only a side effect of his work and to which he never paid much attention. Today, "mesmerism" is considered the same as hypnotism, a fact which Mesmer himself would have bitterly refuted. Hypnotism is a vitally important subject, but in the late eighteenth and early nineteenth centuries mesmerism meant something entirely different. It referred to "Animal Magnetism," the title that Mesmer gave to his discovery.

When he was thirty-one, Mesmer graduated from the University of Vienna with a degree in medicine. By that time he already had two other degrees, including a Ph.D. The subject of his medical thesis is surprising in view of medical thought of his day, but what is even more surprising is that it was accepted. For Mesmer, who was profoundly influenced by the writings of Paracelsus, chose as his topic the influence of planets on the human body. He deeply believed in the essential truth of astrology, but in a spirit of scientific inquiry. He was not concerned with the effects of planetary bodies on circumstances. What interested him was their effect on the human body. As he wrote in his thesis:

> It is obvious that there is hardly any change in the heavenly bodies which does not influence the fluid or firm consistencies of our earth. Can anyone deny, therefore, that animal organisms too, come under these influences. A living creature, too, is part of the earth, and such a creature consists of liquid and firm components, the proportions and equilibrium of which are subtly altered, thus producing effects which are poignantly felt by the creature itself.

Now we know that the life cycles of oysters and certain worms are dependent on moon phases and that sunspots do affect the mental states of humans. We can see that Mesmer was addressing himself to scientific facts. But in his time his theories were only tolerated with amusement.

Mesmer made a great leap, however, by carrying this theory to its logical conclusion. If there was an influence from the stars, then there had to be an influence here on Earth which could interact with it. Out of this grew Mesmer's concept of a universal *fluidum* that penetrated everything, acting as the carrier for the force of animal magnetism, an energy that he quite definitely recognized was not limited to animals.

For about five years after beginning his profession as a physician, Mesmer lived a relatively quiet life, absorbed with his patients and many hobbies, including musical glasses and numerous experiments in physics. Some of these experiments had to do with the application of electricity to healing. Mesmer was still looking for something to justify his theory which held:

*All things in nature possess a particular power which manifests itself by a special action upon other bodies, that is to say, a psycho-dynamic power acting exteriorly, without chemical union, or without being introduced into the interior of the organism.*

Far from being limited to animals, he felt that "all bodies—animals, plants, trees, water, even stones—were impregnated with this magic fluid, which might be spread to a considerable distance."

In 1774, Mesmer heard that a Jesuit priest, a professor at the University of Vienna and a court astrologer for Maria Theresa, was using magnets to produce cures. Since Paracelsus had reported the same possibility two hundred years before, Mesmer became intensely interested and began to work with the priest. While the Jesuit felt the magnet itself to be the healing agent, Mesmer believed it was merely the medium through which a healing fluid acted. Extending his own research, Mesmer applied magnets to some cases of longstanding illness and achieved remarkable cures. He found that the magnets provoked an apparent crisis in symptoms before effecting a cure. "The application of magnetism often increased pain and resulted in an immediate crisis, which was followed by a restful slackness and a gradual recovery of the patient." Further clinical studies convinced him that steel magnets were not the only source of magnetic influence. He found that paper, bread, wool, silk, leather, stones, glass, water, various metals, wood, dogs, humans and virtually everything could seemingly absorb and then emanate a healing force. Eventually he discovered that he was a generator of the force himself and that some patients could be cured by his merely passing his hands over their affected parts.

Mesmer never considered himself to be a spiritual

healer. He knew he was working with a natural phenomena that could be applied by anyone with proper
training. At the same time, he was aware that he was
working primarily with the mind. The healing force
was "psycho-dynamic"; it had to be willed into the
patient and, most important, the patient had to accept
it. A thoroughly skeptical patient could apparently
block the effects of the force. Of course, perhaps
without completely realizing it, Mesmer was working
in large part with the power of suggestion. On the
other hand, he did insist on the importance of a good
rapport being established with the patient, and he
limited his curative attempts to functional disorders,
leaving organic disorders to regular physicians. Also, in
later years he did his best to create a suggestive
atmosphere, using dim lighting, soft music, and even
impressive robes and wands. This aroused the ridicule
of his colleagues, but Mesmer was impervious to that.
He cured his patients. He aroused the anger of other
physicians when, in the face of the prevailing chemical
and mechanical approach to disease (which has lasted
to our own time) he stated, "To the physical causes of
disease must be added moral causes: pride, ambition,
all the vile passions of the human mind, are as many
causes of visible maladies."

Nevertheless, Mesmer's many experiments and successful results were also proof that he was working
with an actual transference of energy of some type.
Suggestion alone could not account for many of the
cures, nor for the extremely short time in which many
of the disorders were eliminated, as some of these were
effected too quickly for suggestion to work.

Most of what has come down to us about Mesmer's
work deals with healing, but it is apparent that he carried out many experiments in the realm of physics as
well. At the request of Dr. Charles Le Roy, President of

the French Academy of Sciences, Mesmer prepared a memorandum about his discoveries which included the following twenty-seven propositions, to which I have added commentaries. The properties of "animal magnetism" described here are the same as those found by other researchers and by my own experiments. These common properties imply that we are dealing with a single energy, *vril:*

1. *"A responsive influence exists between the heavenly bodies, the earth, and all animated bodies."*

This is the basic thesis of astrology. In modern times we recognize gravity, light, radio waves, X-rays and cosmic rays as reaching us from the heavens, so of course the stars and planets influence us. The question is, how much and in what way? The significant difference in Mesmer's concept is that not only do the heavens exert an influence, but the Earth and all her creatures and objects do as well.

2. *"A fluid universally diffused, so continuous as to admit no vacuum, incomparably subtle, and naturally susceptible of receiving, spreading, and communicating all motor disturbance, is the means of this influence."*

Here we have an extremely important point, one which is frequently overlooked or misunderstood. Mesmer makes a clear distinction between the "influence" as such and the means by which it is spread. The universal fluid is the means, the carrier, and must not be confused with the influence itself. There is a remarkable correlation between Mesmer's fluid and influence and the Polynesian concepts of *aka* and *vril.* According to Mesmer, what appears as space between the stars is actually filled with universal fluid. The latest research by astronomers shows that space is not a vacuum, as was once thought, but is "filled" with highly diffused gaseous particles. However, Mesmer would have considered the fluid to be far more subtle than gas, since it has the capacity for penetrating everything. Recently, the theory of a universal ether, comparable to this fluid idea, has been revived in some advanced scientific circles to account for the propogation of energies like light and radio waves. Since these are considered to be vibrations (or waves), there must be a medium to carry them from one place to another, just as the ocean carries waves caused by disturbances from lunar gravity, wind, or earthquakes. This is exactly the role that Mesmer had in mind for the universal fluid.

3. *"This reciprocal action is subject to mechanical laws with which we are not as yet familiar."*
Unfortunately, this statement is as valid today as it was over two hundred years ago. By "reciprocal action" Mesmer meant that if the planets can affect us, then in some way we must have an influence on the planets. Waves striking a shoreline set up counterwaves which flow back in the opposite direction, although much weaker than the original source. The ancient axiom "as above, so below" must have as its corollary "as below, so above." An atomic bomb explosion on Earth might have repercussions that extend far beyond the confines of our atmosphere. This could, just possibly, be the reason for extraterrestrial interest in our affairs, if such actually exists.

4. *"Alternative effects result from this action, which may be considered to be a flux and reflux."*
The "flux and reflux" refers to a continuous flow of movement, like the ocean tides, and confirms the commentary above. "Alternative effects" could refer to both beneficial and harmful effects.

5. *"This reflux is more or less general, more or less special, more or less compound, according to the nature of the causes behind it."*

In other words, the "vibes" given off by our planet may be general (a war), special (the setting off of a hydrogen bomb), or complex (an earthquake or volcanic explosion).

6. *"It is by this action, the most universal which occurs in nature, that the exercise of active relations takes place between the heavenly bodies, the earth, and its constituent parts."*

Here Mesmer simply states his theory that the heavens, the Earth, and everything on the Earth influence each other through continual movements of what he calls the universal fluid.

7. *"The properties of matter and of organic substance depend on this action."*

Logically extending his theory, Mesmer asserts that because everything is always influencing and being influenced, the properties or characteristics of any particular thing are an effect of the combined influences, and not unique to the thing itself.

8. *"The animal body experiences the alternative effects of this agent and is directly affected by its insinuation into the substance of the nerves."*

This is no more than repeating the assertion that we are affected by outside influences. The "substance of the nerves" as receiver for this influence reflects the language of Mesmer's time, since in his day what we would call neuroses were thought to be directly related to the nervous system.

9. *"Properties are displayed, analogous to those of the magnet, particularly in the human body, in which diverse and opposite poles are likewise to be distinguished, and these may be communicated, altered, destroyed, and reinforced. Even the phenomenon of declination may be observed."*

The idea that the human body is polarized is a very old one, found in many different cultures. There is a difference of opinion, however, on the direction of the polarity. Some peoples have believed that the left side acts as one pole and the right side as the other. Others claim the polarity is front and back, and still others claim top and bottom (referring to the head and feet).

One type of experiment strongly indicates a front and back polarity. The subject stands with back to an experimenter who charges himself or herself with *vril* through special breathing or other techniques. The experimenter then raises his or her hands with palms facing the subject's back. In most cases, the subject will be drawn backwards as though by magnetic attraction, *even though no words have been spoken and no hint given of the exact moment the experimenter's hands were raised.* Thus, suggestion does not enter into the picture. In a few cases, the subject feels drawn forward. In these cases an attractive effect is produced when the experimenter stands facing the subject. Not only does this indicate polarity, but a variation in polarity between different subjects.

Another type of experiment lends support to side-to-side polarity. One person touches a charged person or object with the left hand, while the right hand touches or is held near a sensitive subject. The latter reports feeling an outpouring of energy from the person's right hand, and this diminishes sharply when the charged object is released. This also works with the right hand as a receiver and the left as a transmitter, though some sensitives report a difference in the quality of the energy under this arrangement. It is possible that suggestion does play a role here. The same effect can be achieved with people linking hands in a chain.

Because of this current-like effect, an interesting theory analogous to electricity and magnetism has arisen. As electricity and magnetism occur at right angles to each other, it has been proposed that the

front and back polarity is analogous to the magnet,
while the side-to-side polarity is analogous to an electric current. When a charged object is touched by both
feet, an effect can be felt in the head. When the object
is placed on top of the head, it can be felt in the feet.
But if it touches only one foot, subjects report feeling
an outpouring of energy from the opposite foot. How
this fits in with the electromagnetic theory has not
been determined by its proponents.

The properties of the energy of "animal magnetism"
can be communicated, as Mesmer said and as I have
shown above, and they can be altered by the will of the
operator. On some occasions, a person who at first felt
attracted by the experimenter's hands later felt pushed
away by them. The change was brought about by the
experimenter willing it. All effects are apparently
destroyed temporarily by the application of water,
which seems to absorb the energy. This may be the
reason that so many spiritual healers wash their hands
after treating a patient. The effects can be reinforced
by the use of *vril* generators, such as magnets. Mesmer
noted the phenomenon of declination, or the deviation
of the poles in the body from their expected position.
Through my experiments I have been led to believe
that the body has a dynamic, fluctuating polarity,
dependent on outside influences not as yet fully
understood.

> 10. *"This property of the human body which
> renders it susceptible to the influence of the
> heavenly bodies, and of the reciprocal action
> of those which environ it, manifests its analogy
> with the magnet, and this has decided me to adopt
> the term of animal magnetism."*

Now Mesmer has made it even clearer that he distin-
guishes between animal magnetism (*vril*) and the
universal fluid (*aka* or ether). The reciprocal action

here refers to the fact illustrated above that one human body can affect another with animal magnetism. In the rest of the propositions, whenever Mesmer speaks of magnetism he means this particular kind, and not that which is purely a property of minerals.

> *11. "The action and virtue of animal magnetism thus characterized may be communicated to other animate or inanimate bodies. Both these types of bodies, however, vary in their susceptibility."*

I have already discussed communicating energy to animate bodies. I also mentioned "charged objects," and this is what Mesmer referred to in this proposition. He found, and I have too, that an inanimate body such as an ivory statue can apparently absorb *vril* (or animal magnetism) imparted to it by a human, to the point where an energy field is created around it that can be felt by a sensitive subject. This field can have the same effect on another person as the energy emitted by the one who charged it. As Mesmer said, different materials—and people—vary in the amount of *vril* they can absorb. In this proposition we encounter the age-old idea of amulets and talismans as containers of magical power, beyond their use as placebos.

> *12. "This action and virtue may be strengthened and diffused by such bodies."*

An inanimate object can be made into a *vril* generator that works even when far removed from the person who charged it. Some materials, such as various crystals and minerals, seem to act as natural generators which emit *vril* without being charged by a human operator. Lest there be some confusion, I should clarify that a magnet seems to emit both mineral and animal magnetism, somewhat in the way that a light bulb emits both light and heat. *Vril* generators can be used to reinforce or amplify the *vril* in a human being, and

human beings can reinforce or amplify the *vril* in inanimate objects.

*13. "Experiments show that there is a diffusion
of matter, subtle enough to penetrate all bodies
without any considerable loss of energy."*

The "matter" is the universal fluid. This proposition
refers to the fact that *vril* can pass through solid
objects. An interesting experiment is to repeat the
attraction experiment described in the commentary on
proposition 9, but with a sheet of glass or plastic
between the operator and the subject. The only difference in the effects is one of time. Assuming that *vril*
requires universal fluid as a carrier, the only way to
explain the action of *vril* through solids is to assume
that the fluid can penetrate all bodies.

*14. "Its [the animal magnetism's] action takes place
at a remote distance without the aid of any inter-
mediary substance."*

We call this the "induction effect." In experiments
more fully described in another chapter, I transmitted
*vril* to subjects in another room and even many miles
away. An analogy can be made with radio receivers
and transmitters, especially since a mental tuning or
channeling process is required.

*15. "It is, like light, increased and reflected by
mirrors."*

Mesmer discovered that directing animal magnetism
toward the mirror image of a subject affected him or
her exactly as if it were directed to the person. I have
not carried out adequate experiments to test this thesis,
but the effect has been reported from other sources.

*16. "It is communicated, spread, and increased by
sound."*

Sound, in the form of music or chanting, has been used
since time immemorial for "raising the vibrations" of a

group of people or even an individual. The sound itself does seem to increase one's supply of *vril*, as long as it is the right kind of sound. Group or individual chanting of the mystical word "AUM" can be tremendously beneficial for mental and physical health, particularly when done on a rising scale. One experiences a real "high" that lasts for hours afterward. In a system of healing called "Toning," vocal sounds of different pitches are directed toward a patient or intoned by the patient, and some remarkable cures are claimed. My personal experience shows that even singing or humming can amplify one's *vril*.

    *17. "This magnetic virtue may be accumulated, concentrated, and transported."*

One way of accumulating *vril* is by special breathing and visualization techniques. Some of these are complicated, but a simple form is to sit quietly for a few moments and visualize yourself surrounded by a golden light (representing *vril*). Then take four slow, deep breaths. On the inhale, visualize the *vril* coming into your body. On the exhale, feel it being stored either in your solar plexus or your head. This is an excellent pick-me-up whenever you are fatigued or want to increase mental alertness. You are using imagination and suggestion, but you accumulate a real supply of *vril*, which can easily be felt as a sensation of tingling, a current or increased warmth.

    Of course, *vril* can also be accumulated, concentrated and transported in inanimate objects, as noted. You can test this by performing the breathing technique described above, only instead of storing the *vril* on the exhale, extend your hands over a glass of water and will the *vril* into it as you let out your breath. If you have accumulated enough *vril*, and if your taste buds have not been desensitized by too much tobacco or alcohol, you will be able to taste a definite difference between your treated water and a glass of untreated water. The treated water will have become "magnetized," to use an old expression from Mesmer's day.

*18. "I have said that animated bodies are not all equally susceptible; in a few instances they have such an opposite property that their presence is enough to destroy all the effects of magnetism upon other bodies."*

Plants thrive for people who have a "green thumb" in ways that cannot be explained by mere physical care. They can take plants that others have abandoned and restore them to sprightly life in a very short time. But there are also people with "brown thumbs" for whom nothing will grow right. Their very presence seems to cause plants to wilt. People with green thumbs emit a beneficial form of *vril;* those with brown thumbs emit, unconsciously for the most part, a form of *vril* which is detrimental, at least to plants. There are also people whose presence is highly unsettling to other people. They cause nervousness or depression in others just by being around, like the little character with the black cloud in old Li'l Abner comic strips. Still others seem to drain one of energy when they are close by, as if they are sucking it up. In occult lore, they are called "psychic vampires," but that implies conscious intent, which is rarely the case. However, probably instead of actually being drained of energy, the apparent victims are merely reacting to a negative influence, as they would to any stress-producing source of energy.

Mesmer proposed that this negative energy is not just the opposite pole of animal magnetism, but a kind of "anti-animal magnetism," with its own polarity. It could be the source of evil and black magic. Perhaps it is also the cause of death by old age and the so-called "virtue" by which poisonous substances are created. On the other hand, it may not be a negative aspect of

*vril* at all, but an effect of too much intensity, or of a
pattern of disharmony, like discordant notes, that the
*vril* simply energizes.

 20. *"The magnet, whether natural or artificial, is
 like other bodies susceptible of animal magnetism,
 and even of the opposite virtue; in neither case
 does its action on fire and on the needle suffer any
 change, and this shows that the principle of animal
 magnetism differs fundamentally from that of
 mineral magnetism."*

Mesmer states in this proposition what I have stated
already: that magnetism as we know it and *vril* are not
identical. Note, however, that he says a magnet may be
imbued with anti-*vril*. A simple change in polarity may
make differences in effects. Some people report that
holding one end of a magnet causes a headache, but
holding the other end is beneficial. This is probably
more a case of personal polarity rather than an indication of the presence of anti-*vril*. In all my years of experience and experimentation, I have found nothing to
indicate the existence of anti-*vril*. Any negative effects
have been easily explained by overintensity of the
energy and/or stress resistance on the part of subjects.

 I was intrigued with Mesmer's statement about the
action of a magnet on fire. The only relation we know
of between a magnet and fire is that sufficient heat can
destroy a magnet's properties. But this did not seem to
be what Mesmer was talking about. So I lit a candle
and experimented with a powerful, small magnet.
When the magnet was brought to within a few inches
of the flame, the flame seemed to bend slightly toward
the magnet. When it was brought to within a few frac-
tions of an inch, the flame flickered and its center bent
sharply toward the magnet. A piece of brass produced
no effect at a distance of a few inches. Close up it
caused no flickering, but the middle of the flame bent

sharply *away* from the brass. A finger produced the same effects as the magnet. Glass caused the same effect as brass, while a powerful *vril* generator called a Manabloc caused effects like the magnet and finger from over an inch away. Here are more indications that *vril* is an active force.

*21. "This system sheds new light upon the nature of fire and of light, as well as on the theory of attraction, of flux and reflux, of the magnet and of electricity."*

At least it allows us to look at those phenomena in a new light.

*22. "It teaches us that the magnet and artificial electricity have, with respect to diseases, properties common to many other agents presented to us by nature, and that if the use of these has achieved some useful results, they are due to animal magnetism."*

Mesmer made a very important statement here, and one that has been borne out by many experiments. It implies that he experimented with electricity to effect some successful cures and that the results he obtained were identical to those produced with the magnet, as well as by the laying-on of hands. The statement also implies that whenever electricity or magnetism is present, *vril* is also present.

Whether *vril* is a by-product of electromagnetism or vice versa is an interesting field for speculation, but one we do not have space to pursue. What we do know is that *vril* is indeed present when electromagnetism is present, for the same effects have been obtained with electromagnetic devices as with hands, pyramids, oracs, manaboxes and other things described in later chapters. This corresponds, of course, to the Law of the Elephant (if it looks like an elephant, acts like an elephant, feels like an elephant and smells like an elephant, it probably *is* an elephant). But because *vril* is not easily measurable and is found in so many different sources, orthodox science has so far refused to accept the implications.

> *23. "These facts show, in accordance with the practical rules I am about to establish, that this principle will cure nervous diseases directly, and other diseases indirectly."*

No comment needed.

> *24. "By its aid the physician is enlightened as to the use of medicine, and may render its action more perfect, and he can provoke and direct salutary crises so as to control them completely."*

This is actually a conciliatory statement intended to convince physicians that the use of animal magnetism would not be a threat to their regular practice. However, *vril* was then and still is too nonphysical to be comfortable for most physicians.

> *25. "In communicating my method, I shall, by a new theory of matter, demonstrate the universal usefulness of the principle I seek to establish."*

The theory is unimportant to our present study.

> *26. "With this knowledge, the physician may judge with certainty of the origin, nature, and progress of diseases, however complicated they may be; he may hinder their progress and accomplish their cure without exposing the patient to dangerous and troublesome consequences, irrespective of age, temperament, and sex. Even women in a state of pregnancy, and during parturition, may reap the same advantage."*

Prescribing curtailed use of drugs is one of the things that got Mesmer into deep trouble with his colleagues, who were inveterate pill-pushers. "Dangerous and troublesome consequences" referred to the effects of drugs, and drugs were the mainstay of the medical profession of his day. Sound familiar? At one time he wrote that the unfortunate habit of physicians "of continually giving drugs will stand in the way of animal magnetism for a long time." How long he could never have guessed. Yet Mesmer was a good doctor and an eminently practical man. He was not against drugs as such. He also wrote, "Drugs for internal and external use must be sparingly applied, but they must not be discarded altogether."

*27. "This doctrine will, finally, enable the physician to decide upon the health of every individual, and upon the presence of the diseases to which he may be exposed. In this way the art of healing may be brought to absolute perfection."*

This is a high hope, but one that was not brought to fruition in Mesmer's day, nor yet in ours. Mesmer's colleagues were well satisfied with the art of healing as it was progressing for them. They were afraid of him, his theories and especially his successful results. They succeeded eventually in driving him into an obscure exile, but they could not prevent the spread of his ideas. However, as so often happens, his followers either distorted his discoveries or emphasized only certain aspects to the detriment of the whole. At least one fortunate outcome is the discovery of hypnotherapy, but even its practitioners had to fight for nearly a century to gain recognition from the medical establishment.

### The Power of Magnets and Animal Magnetism

It is one thing to record the belief that magnets aid healing as presented by a nineteenth century doctor whose colleagues called him a quack and a charlatan. It is quite another to claim that magnets can have an effect on us today. But they do.

Magnetism is used to heal today, but its acceptance is facing the same kind of hostility that ruined Mesmer. There are published studies showing that a device called the Diapulse machine, which emits pulsed, high-frequency electromagnetic radio waves, induces dramatic healing of such illnesses as sinusitis and impaired circulation in the legs. The machine does nothing except to create an electromagnetic field which penetrates into the body seven inches, and this got the producer company in trouble with the FDA. It is "common knowledge" that a magnetic field can have no effect on living tissue, so the FDA designated the Diapulse claims as sheer quackery, banned interstate distribution and blocked further research. The "common knowledge," however, is completely at variance with successful tests carried out at hospitals and laboratories in Great Britain, New York, Philadelphia and elsewhere. In rigorously controlled clinical studies, use of the Diapulse resulted in outstandingly successful treatment of serious ankle sprains, chronic lesions, painful sinus inflammation and the healing of wounds. In one case, the need for drugs was reduced 50 to 100 percent. This might, in fact, suggest a clue to the reasons for FDA hostility. If Mesmer could see us now, he might smile a bitter smile.

High-powered electromagnetism is not the only kind that will affect living tissue. In a series of experiments with ten subjects I tested reactions to a magnet being passed over their arms, hands, face and head. One subject felt nothing at all; four subjects felt either a cool-breeze sensation or a tingling in the area of the wrists and palms only; three subjects also felt this on their bare arms; and two subjects experienced the sensations on all parts of the body tested. Suggestion was ruled out because the subjects were blindfolded and could not see where the magnets were being held. None of them had ever noticed any sensation from the proximity of magnets before. It is my contention that this is because they had not paid attention to it.

Canadian studies show that many seeds germinate and grow faster if they have been exposed to a magnetic field before planting, with some seeds growing about five times faster than unexposed seeds in the first forty-eight hours. The scientists reporting the study actually recommended that home gardeners try exposing their seed to a magnetic field before planting. Since my experiments have accomplished similar results with materials other than magnets, I am led back to Mesmer's conclusion that the active force is not mineral magnetism, but something else—*vril.*

Mesmer deserves an honored place in the history of research into earth energies. I hope that one day he will be generally recognized for his accomplishments, and not for what others did in his name.

# 3
# The Odic Force and Reichenbach

Except to students of *vril* research, the name of Baron von Reichenbach is hardly known today. Yet, in the early nineteenth century it was well known in scientific circles throughout Europe. Reichenbach, whose scientific credentials were quite sound, was at first highly regarded as an authority on meteorites and the discoverer of creosote. However, after he turned his attention to the study of what he called "od," he attracted irate attacks from scientific colleagues, and even his friends abandoned him. Though he performed thousands of well-documented experiments concerning od and many of his subjects were themselves scientists, the results he obtained were ignored or scorned. This was primarily because they ran counter to the conventional wisdom of the day and for his data he relied on "sensitives," persons regarded as having extended sensory perception. In addition, so much of what he discovered coincided with Mesmer's "animal magnetism" that Reichenbach became a victim of guilt by association. Since mesmerism had already been discarded by the scientific establishment, it was "natural" to discard the theory of od as well. Reichenbach tried in vain to dissociate his work from that of Mesmer, even to the

**38**

point of wrongly accusing the latter of confusing
animal magnetism with ordinary magnetism, but that
did not heal the rift with his colleagues.

A curious trait of Western scientists and researchers
is their desire to rename *vril* every time it is rediscovered. Perhaps it is egotism, or ignorance of what
others have discovered, or even a sincere belief that the
discovery is unique. The fact remains that in Europe
and America in the last two hundred years some thirty
or more different names have been given to what appears to be the same thing. To this list Reichenbach
added the word "od." His description of the etymology
of this word is quite interesting:

> *For heat, electricity and light, there are, to a
> certain degree, insulators; but I have not yet
> been able to contrive anything of this kind in
> forming an appellation suited to manifold scien-
> tific applications. Va denotes, in Sanscrit, to
> breathe; in Latin, vado. In Icelandic, vada
> means I go quickly, I haste on, I stream forth.
> From it is derived Wodan, in the ancient Ger-
> man, expressing the notion of an all-pervading
> power; it is changed in several idioms of the
> German into Wodan, Odan, etc.; everywhere
> signifying a power penetrating everything,
> which at last is personified in Odin, a deity of
> the ancient Germans. Od is, therefore, the vocal
> expression of a dynamid, subtly pervading and
> streaming with an irresistible force through
> everything in nature.*

Remember that Mesmer mentioned the all-
pervasiveness of his animal magnetism, and you will
meet this concept again. A decided advantage of
Reichenbach's name for it is that "od" can be used
both as a prefix, as in odic, and as a suffix, as in

"heliod" (od from the sun). It is much more efficient than such terms as "psychotronic energy" or "animal magnetism" or even *vril*.

## Magnets and Od

Reichenbach experimented with "magnetod," the odic force emanating from magnets. The baron made no secret of the fact that he was stimulated by the work of Mesmer, and it was in order to prove or disprove Mesmer's claims that he first began his research. Like Mesmer, he found that many people could distinctly feel various sensations when a magnet was passed over their bodies without actually touching them.

> *[The sensations were] rather disagreeable than pleasant, and combined with a slight sensation either of cold or warmth, resembling a cool or gently warm breath of air, which the patients imagine to blow softly upon them. Sometimes they feel sensations of drawing, pricking, or creeping; some complain of sudden attacks of headache. Not only women, but men in the very prime of life, are found distinctly suscepti- ble of this influence; in children it is sometimes very active.*

Note how similar this report is to my own findings described in Chapter 2. Curiously, I discovered that the same person may experience different sensations on different occasions. The first time he or she may feel a tingling, the next a cool breeze, the next warmth. I do not know as yet whether this is a result of a change in the source, the subject, orientation or the environment, although some materials tend to produce a particular type of sensation more often than others.

Mesmer was primarily interested in the healing

qualities of energy, but Reichenbach was more concerned with its nature. This led him to perform some unusual experiments with astounding results. Finding certain people sensitive to tactile sensations produced by the magnet, Reichenbach wondered if, in absolute darkness, they might not receive visual sensations. This hunch paid off handsomely. Working first with a girl subject to cataleptic fits, he discovered that she could see light emanating from the poles of a magnet while in a room so completely dark that no one else could see anything. When an armature was placed on the poles, however, the light disappeared. What the girl described was more than just light; it was a moving, shifting flame:

> The whole appearance was more delicate and beautiful than that of common fire; the light was far purer, almost white, sometimes intermingled with iridescent colors, the whole resembling the light of the sun more than that of a fire. The distribution of the light in rays was not uniform; in the middle of the edges of the horseshoe they were more crowded and brilliant than toward the corners, but at the corners they were collected in tufts, which projected further than the rest of the rays.

Highly encouraged, Reichenbach continued his experiments with other sensitives, many in apparent excellent health. Their observations were all confirmatory. According to their degree of sensitivity, they saw either a faint glow at the poles or magnificent fiery blossoms of flame resembling a giant iris. Using a powerful horseshoe magnet with both poles pointed upward, Reichenbach's sensitives reported that the flames from the two poles did not intermingle, but remained distinctly separate. Both flames were "filled with numberless small spots, white-hot, shining and forming altogether a column of light as big as a man." The term "white-hot" must be taken as descriptive, since no mention is made of an actual temperature recording. Gradually, Reichenbach determined that the north pole of a magnet seemed to exude a bluish flame associated with a cool feeling, while the color streaming from the south pole was yellow-reddish, associated with warmth.

The column of light rose to the ceiling and formed an illuminated circle about six feet in diameter. As the sensitives continued their stay in the darkened room, the light seemed to become stronger, until they could discern objects and people quite distant from the magnet itself. Quite interestingly, this light would move like a candle flame if one breathed into it, and a hand placed into it would throw a shadow.

If the opposite poles of two magnets were brought together, the flames were seen to penetrate each other undisturbed. But if one magnet was stronger than the other, the flame of the stronger would clear the weaker. Reichenbach also found that the light from the magnet could be focused with a magnifying glass and reflected by a mirror.

A fascinating discovery in relation to the magnet was what Reichenbach called "the rainbow of od." A great number of sensitives during thousands of experiments reported a spectrum of colors appearing within the blue or yellow-tinted flames of the poles of the magnets. When not disturbed by breath or motion, these colors arranged themselves in an orderly rainbow sequence, with red at the bottom and dark blue and violet-red at the top. The top color "died gradually away into a smoke-like vapor." The whole spectrum of colors was intermingled with sparkling points of light.

In one series of experiments, Reichenbach used a bar

magnet with a cross-section of one square inch. The south pole pointing upwards produced the red-tinted spectrum, and the north pole turned upwards produced the blue-tinted spectrum. With the north pole still pointing up, Reichenbach placed a pointed iron cap upon it. The emanation of light "became thinner, more lucid and higher, but the succession of rainbow-colors continued." When the baron placed a two-pointed cap on the magnet, one point exuded a blue flame and the other a yellow-reddish one. A four-pointed cap produced four different colored flames, one from each point: blue, yellow, red and grayish-white. The spectrum effect was no longer evident.

Turning the magnet on its vertical axis produced a great surprise, for the colors remained stationary. In other words, they did not change position along with the metal points. When the point which had emitted a yellow flame arrived at the position of the original blue flame, it emitted blue. All the other points produced the same effect, as if the flames derived from an exterior source. Reichenbach soon determined that the "blue light appeared each time on the tooth directed northward, the yellow on that directed westward, the red southward and the grayish-white eastward."

Next he replaced the tooth cap with a foot-sqaure iron plate. One flame sprang from each corner in the same relative colors as above, but emanating horizontally instead of vertically. When the plate was turned 45 degrees from the compass points, mixed colors appeared: green toward the northwest, orange toward the southwest, grayish-red toward the southeast and violet toward the northeast.

Finally, Reichenbach had a hollow ball of iron constructed and suspended it in his darkroom by a silk cord. Inside he arranged a vertical iron rod wound with six strands of copper wire. He attached the rod to a voltaic battery of zinc and silver plates.

> *[The sensitives] saw the suspended ball step-*
> *ping forth from the darkness, clad in various col-*
> *ors. The whole surface was glittering in*
> *rainbow light. The scales of the ball toward the*
> *north were blue, those toward the northwest*
> *green, those toward the west yellow, toward*
> *the southwest orange, toward the south red,*
> *toward the southeast grayish-red, toward the*
> *east gray, toward the northeast reddish stripes*
> *mixed with blue recurred again. The colors*
> *were visibly forming delicate lines one beside*
> *another, separated by others darker. The whole*
> *ball was wrapt in a delicately shining sphere of*
> *vapor. The top half of the globe has a bluish*
> *cast over all its colors, while over the bottom*
> *half was a cast of reddish light.*

Another description must be quoted to get the full effect:

> *On the top, where was the north pole of the*
> *electro-magnet, arose palm-high over the globe,*
> *an illuminated column of light playing into*
> *blue, then curving in all directions like an open*
> *umbrella, and running down all around the ball*
> *at a distance of two to three inches from it.*
> *From the other pole, the south pole, on the*
> *lower part arose similar sheaves of lustre,*
> *though of reddish color, all around the ball.*
> *Both these shining phenomena continued fall-*
> *ing asunder, and died away before reaching the*
> *equator of the globe.*

Being familiar with terrestrial magnetism, Reichenbach contended that the northern lights would probably be found to be a manifestation of od.

Such a display of colors was repeatedly described as a spectacular sight. These experiments should be widely duplicated in our day so that we do not have to rely solely on reports over a hundred years old. It is noteworthy that some clairvoyants today claim to see the human body surrounded by a rainbow display of colors. The way the colors vary according to the points of the compass needs to be studied seriously. The polarization may furnish important clues as to the different uses and effects of the energy. Reichenbach encouraged duplication, but said,

> I must caution you against omitting any precautions for getting absolute darkness, and for accustoming the eyes of the performer to the latter for some hours; otherwise your observer could see nothing, you would operate in vain, and the truthfulness of my statements would run the risk of being suspected, undeservedly.

### Crystals and Od

The work with magnets comprised only one part of Reichenbach's experimentation. He found, for instance, that crystals emit od also, which he promptly labeled "crystallod." For most of these experiments he used a large quartz crystal, again in a darkened room. The sensitive reported:

> [The] whole body [of the crystal] glowed throughout with a delicate light, and . . . over its upper point was streaming forth a light as large as a hand, or the palm of a hand, blue, in constant motion, sometimes scintillating, of tulip form, dissolving in its upper part into a delicate vapor.

The end of the crystal which had been attached to the matrix invariably emitted a yellowish-red vapor. Here again we have the phenomena of polarity. The blue end was always said to be cool and the red-yellow end warmish. I have experimented with a small quartz crystal on a number of subjects with the same effects.

Crystals of various sorts are known to exhibit electrical properties under certain conditions, as are magnets. It might, therefore, easily be supposed that we are dealing merely with some unknown properties of electricity itself. However, a number of experiments seem to refute this. For one thing, Reichenbach found that *all* crystals exhibited the presence of the odic force, with or without the presence of conditions conducive to the production of electricity. The application of heat, which excites an electrical effect in tourmaline, for instance, caused no perceptible difference in the emission of od from a crystal of that substance. Many experiments confirmed this finding, including those with magnets and other materials. Od was always found in conjunction with electricity and magnetism, but it was found without them, too.

Reichenbach found an interesting relation between the od polarity and the crystalline structure. Crystallographers know that crystals possess several axes, both main and secondary. Using a variety of crystals, Reichenbach had his sensitives locate the points that gave off the greatest concentration of odic force. All of them agreed that it was the location of the odic poles: "The axes and poles always coincided with the axes and poles of crystallography, and thus it became more than probable that the crystallic force takes part in (if it does not wholly effect) the construction of crystals." Reichenbach also noted that crystals grow in any direction, without regard to terrestrial magnetism, and yet they still emit the od in the direction of growth. Still, the colors noted arrange themselves in accordance with the compass points. There is a great mystery to unravel here.

## Polarity Between Substances

Reichenbach discovered not only a polarity within various substances, but a polarity between substances as well. In the course of his experiments, he found that many sensitives responded with an apparent temperature sensation of unpleasant warmth and prickling to some substances and of pleasant coolness to others. All in all, Reichenbach tested his sensitives with six hundred different substances with puzzling results. Many materials felt warm to the touch, but seemed to emit a cool breeze when placed some distance away. Some produced unpleasant sensations when alone, but pleasant ones when combined with other substances.

Reichenbach also found that the od could apparently be made to flow from one substance to another. To test this flowing effect myself, I used two crystals—one of aquamarine and the other of ulexite. I had particular reasons for choosing these two. Aquamarine is a form of beryl, from which we get beryllium, a substance used in atomic research because it emits neutrons. Ulexite is a form of boron, used to line atomic reactors because it absorbs neutrons. I had my subjects hold a crystal in each hand and report the effects. Most reported feeling the sensation of a current flowing up the arms and through the chest. Reports varied as to whether the current flowed to or from a particular crystal. One person, with a history of chest tumors, reported feeling a warm, tingling sensation in the chest only. Another reported no current, but felt a temperature difference in each hand. Objective observation showed that the temperature of the hands was indeed different from the temperature in the rest of the body, the hand holding the aquamarine being cooler and the other warmer. One subject reported no sensations at all, yet the temperature of the crystals themselves had changed. The ulexite grew warmer and the aquamarine cooler. Another "flow test" involved a strong magnet and activated charcoal. In this case, the magnet was suspended four inches above the charcoal, both poles pointing downward. All subjects reported a clear sensation of warmth when passing their hands between the two poles, and some felt a resistance, as if the air between the poles was somewhat viscous.

## Subjective Effects

Reichenbach made many notes about the way different substances affected sensitives physiologically. Besides the subjective sensations, there were objective reactions of convulsions, painless tonic spasms. headaches, pain relief, irritability and pacification, to name a few. Reichenbach's descriptions run to many detailed pages, so here I mention only a few of my own findings with several dozen subjects, more for the sake of stimulating research than of making an exhaustive report. The subjects either held the crystals, meditated with them, or placed them under their pillows while sleeping. They reported that clear quartz crystal had a pleasantly calming effect, but when discolored by radiation it was highly energizing. Sodalite, a component of lapis lazuli, usually caused a feeling of relaxation when held. However, in one instance, a piece of sodalite tested by several subjects caused insomnia and nervousness. I do not know how it differed from other pieces purchased in the same lot, but after being handled for a total of about three hours it had changed from a rather bright blue (the normal shade) to nearly black. None of the other specimens have reacted in this way so far. My only explanation is that some impurity in the stone must have reacted chemically with something on the skin of one of the subjects, but this does not explain the physiological reactions. Jasper, expecially orbicular jasper, had a very calming and soothing effect. In the metals, copper was stimulating, aluminum soothing, and iron/steel somewhere in between.

## Od and the Human Body

Like Mesmer, Reichenbach soon found, to his astonishment, that his own body emitted od. In the dark, rays of light were seen to stream from his fingertips to a distance of several inches, and his body appeared clothed in a vapor-like mist. Because the fingertip streams exhibited the same properties as the flames of the crystals and magnets, Reichenbach naturally concluded that the same force was at work and that it was this force that produced the beneficial effects of the laying-on of hands. It is remarkable that the sensitives reported an appearance of light around the fingers that is astoundingly similar to that recorded today by Kirlian photography. Several observers stated that "fiery brushes of light issue from the points of the fingers of healthy men, in the same manner as from the poles of crystals."

The last chapter discussed the old tradition of body polarity and Mesmer's statement in regard to it. Reichenbach, too, rediscovered this phenomenon. He first noticed that many people have difficulty sleeping on their left side, and that some people become distinctly uncomfortable, even ill, if forced to sit, stand or sleep in a particular direction. After much experimentation, he determined that the human body is polarized left to right. He called the different poles "od-positive" and "od-negative." Unfortunately, his own terminology confused him, and sometimes he referred to the right as positive and at other times as negative. The blue color and the north end of a magnet he usually called negative. I will accept his description of the left side of the body as positive for now in order to explain some of his theories.

As similar poles of a magnet repel each other, so similar odic poles cause unpleasantness and discomfort. The reason many people cannot sleep on their left side, according to Reichenbach, is because the earth is od-positive, forming an antagonistic relationship with the od-positive left side and resulting in uneasiness. For the same reason, many people cannot support a long stay in a church where the altar is at the east end. But this does not explain why so many religions emphasize facing east while praying. Since this is found in numerous groups that have no "holy city" to turn to, it must be more than a sign of geographical recognition. At the same time, it would seem to be contrary to nature if Reichenbach is right. I cannot believe that sensitive religous leaders would pick an orientation that would be upsetting. Reichenbach probably overlooked something. He apparently did not agree with Mesmer that the poles of the body can change. According to ancient Chinese tradition, however, there is one polarity in the morning and another for the evening; one for the waxing moon and another for the waning. These variations are taken into account in the practice of acupuncture.

Reichenbach did discover a front-to-back polarity. To his sensitives, the forehead emitted cold, or negative, od, and the occiput, or back of the head, positive. These coincide with the traditional seats of the conscious and subconscious, respectively. With the help of a graph and twenty-four-hour testing. Reichenbach showed that the odic emission from the forehead began to increase at a rapid rate at sunrise, reaching its height just after sunset. Then it declined to a low point around 4:00 A.M. and rose again with the sun. The emission from the occiput, on the other hand, reached its high point at about 3:00 A.M. and dropped rapidly toward sunrise. Then it continued in a gradual decline till hitting its lowest point in late afternoon. On a graph, the rises and falls of front and back show an almost exact opposition. Interestingly, the paths crossed at midnight and sunrise, two times well known to be favorable for psychic perception. Here is research that may lead to further valuable experimental work.

## Luminosity of the Body

The third body polarity that Reichenbach discovered corresponds to an idea found in occult and oriental theory. Sensitives noted a spectrum of colors, much like that described for the magnet, ascending from the genital region, where it was reddish, to the top of the head, where it was violet. This corresponds to yoga philosophy concerning the colors of the chakras, psychic transducers of prana, which are located near the physical endocrine glands. The whole body glows to some sensitive eyes, says Reichenbach:

*Human beings are luminous almost all over the surface of their bodies, but especially on the hands, the palms of the hands, the points of the fingers, the eyes, different parts of the head, the pit of the stomach, the toes, etc. Flame-like streams of light of relatively greater intensity flow from the points of all the fingers, in a straight direction from where they are stretched out.*

Someday, all of this may be photographed. In the meantime it is interesting to note how the luminosity corresponds to information about body energy output received from other sources. The hands, notably the palms, have a high intensity, and these are used in manual healing. The emanations from the tips of the fingers show up in many folk tales of wizards who could wreak destruction or evoke healing by pointing their finger at something. It has long been a tradition that certain people could emit a beam of power from their eyes. Dowser Verne Cameron, whose work is discussed in detail in Chapters 6 and 7, located and measured this beam with his Aurameter, and also located beams issuing from the temples. The pit of the stomach, region of the solar plexus, is considered an energy focal point in many cultures.

## Od from the Sun and Moon

The basic tenet of astrology is that the heavenly bodies emit a power that affects the minds and circumstances of human beings. Some possible confirmation of this may have been unearthed with Reichenbach's discovery of heliod and lunod. The first experiment of this kind was conducted on a cloudless day. A sensitive subject held one end of an eleven-yard copper wire indoors, and the other end was in the sunshine outside. The subject felt a barely perceptible emanation of the odic force, to which she had become sensitized through work with magnets and crystals. Then Reichenbach attached the outside end of the wire to a copper plate four inches square and, after allowing the subject to get adjusted, placed the square directly in the sun. Immediately, the subject gave a cry of pleasure. She felt a strong emanation as warmth which ascended through the arm to the head. But an unexpected result was a simultaneous sensation of coolness, which produced an experience of strengthening refreshment throughout the limbs of the subject. She described herself as greatly relieved and cheered by it. "Heat and cold were felt together." The cool sensation disappeared when the plate was placed in the shade, only to return when the sun again struck it. If the sun's rays were allowed to strike the plate obliquely, the effect was lessened, and was stronger when they struck the plate vertically. The same experience occurred regardless of the time of day or the month of the year. It is interesting to note how closely this corresponds with the requirements for sunlight on solar energy panels.

Modifying the experiment, Reichenbach found that the same effect from sunlight was produced whether the wire was attached to copper, iron, zinc, lead, silver, gold, brass, linen, wool, cotton, silk, glass, porcelain, stone, wood, water, lamp-oil, alcohol, sulphur and everything the Baron took into his head to try. Foregoing the wire, Reichenbach placed a glass of water in the sun for twenty minutes and gave it to the subject, who thought it had been treated with a magnet. He had already determined that the taste and effects of a simple glass of water could be altered by magnets, crystals and the human hand. The sunlight produced the same effects, and obviously the same force was involved.

Many of Reichenbach's experiments confirmed the fact that being exposed to the sunlight greatly amplifies the odic properties of magnets, crystals, metals and the human body itself. Later experiments proved that virtually every material could be a conductor of this force. Luminosity experiments, using a wire with one end in a darkened room and the other end attached to various objects in the sunlight, produced the same effects as with previously tested substances.

Since sunlight contains the whole spectrum of colors, Reichenbach wanted to find out whether a particular

color rather than the combination produced the effect.
For this purpose he set up a prism and passed the
outer end of a wire, not visible to the subject, across
the various colors. The results with many subjects were
uniform:

*Violet blue and blue were the principal seat of the*
*solar agreeable influence, and of that reviving*
*coolness which diffused itself throughout the body*
*of the [subject]; consequently, that part of the spec-*
*trum in which exists the least intensity of light.*

On the other hand:

*The sensation of heating of the wire, although it*
*was some six yards long, increased continually*
*from the middle, from yellow to orange, so that it*
*was most distinct and deep in the red. Here we*
*find the maximum of the heating rays; the true*
*warmth of which, however, was far from being*
*able to reach the [subject].*

Quite a few people today are convinced of the efficacy
of color healing, especially the use of the blues. It is
well known that colors can affect moods, but except for
their application to environments in mental institutions,
hospitals and workplaces, their use in actual healing
has not been generally accepted, though it has been
studied.

It was a natural step for Reichenbach to try his next
investigations with the moon. Experiments conducted in
the same manner as with the sun showed conclusively
that the moon was another source of this strange
power. However, instead of refreshing coolness, the
sensation was one of warmth only. Possibly this is
because moonlight is polarized and reflected. This
is borne out by the fact that candlelight produced

exactly the same responses as sunlight, though in
weaker form. At any rate, here was evidence of
something definite coming from heavenly bodies that
was neither ordinary light nor gravity.

To test some of Reichenbach's findings in regard to
the sun, I drew identical glasses of water from a tap.
I placed one of them on a counter in a room and the
other in late afternoon sunlight for a period of twenty
minutes. This water normally had a strong chlorine
taste. At the end of the time period, and after making
sure any temperature difference was minimal, the
water was given to five subjects to test their reactions.
All but one immediately detected a marked difference
in taste between the two, and they preferred the water
that had been in the sun. One said it tasted like it had
been distilled, and another asked whether it had been
charged on a *vril* generator. They all remarked on the
absence of the chlorine taste. It is well known that
something in sunlight breaks down the chlorine, but
sunlight also changes water in other ways, perhaps as
an effect of *vril*. My family and I have used "sun-
charged" water for many years to increase the well-
being of plants, animals and people. The water and
glass combination is a special factor discussed in a
later chapter.

## Friction and Od

Friction is apparently another source of the odic force.
Reichenbach had his sensitives hold one end of a
copper wire and attached the other end to various
materials which he then caused to be rubbed. The subjects reported effects at the far end of the wire similar
to those exhibited by other proven sources. The blade
of a saw being used for cutting a piece of wood seemed

to glow in the dark with a red light as if with heat, and little flames sprouted from each tooth. Zinc rubbed with copper produced a few sparks, but zinc on zinc and copper on copper emitted very little light. Charcoal when rubbed appeared to glow with red deep in the material, and sugar caused quite a show of light. Glass became fiery at the point of contact, as did porcelain. Gypsum on gypsum produced no light at all. Pains were taken to ensure that the results were not caused by ordinary static electricity.

It is well known among healers that friction of the hands induces a greater flow of the healing energy. A simple experiment produces readily discernible sensations for most people, but not all. Rub your hands very quickly together for a few moments, then hold them with palms facing and about a foot apart. It may help to cup the hands slightly. Move your hands gently toward and away from each other. If you are the slightest bit sensitive you will feel, apart from the tingling, a kind of pressure against your palms when you bring them towards each other. It will be somewhat like the effect of two similar magnetic poles being brought together. This is a tangible manifestation of od, or *vril*. The feeling may be extremely slight, so do not be disappointed if you do not feel it the first time.

### Chemical Action and Od

"Chemod" refers to the odic force produced by chemical action, another source discovered by Reichenbach. With his handy wire, he connected his subject to a glass of water into which had been dissolved bicarbonate of soda. Then he dropped a pinch of tartaric acid into the solution. As soon as, and as long as, the decomposition took place, the subject acknowledged the same sensations as caused by magnets, crystals and hands. Iron in sulphuric acid and common salt in water and wine had the same effect. Other combinations confirmed the finding that chemical action produces odic force. By placing a glass of water inside another container in which chemical action was taking place, Reichenbach succeeded in "magnetizing" the water, as he had done by sunlight. Visual effects attesting to the presence of od were observed in every case. With great insight Reichenbach observed that digestion, a chemical process taking place within the body, must also be a source of the life energy to the individual. Respiration, too, is a chemical action, and odic force is a result. Could it be that the age-old idea of breathing prana from the atmosphere is no more than a poetic description of enhanced od production taking place in the lungs as the increase in oxygen causes a chemical reaction in the blood?

The discovery that chemical action produces od led Reichenbach to some remarkable conclusions and a possible explanation for the specters that seem to haunt cemeteries. Reasoning that such apparitions might be caused merely by the chemical decomposition of the dead bodies, Reichenbach brought a brave and highly sensitive girl to a graveyard late at night. True to his expectations, she saw luminous vapors waving over the graves, extending only the length of the grave's mound. "She described the appearance as less like a clear flame than a dense vapor-like mass of fire, intermediate between flame and mist." Some of them were as high as her neck. The girl was not at all frightened as the forms she saw were so like the ones she had often perceived emanating from other substances in Reichenbach's house. She walked right into some of them. When she placed her hand into a form, she said it was like bringing it into a "dense fiery cloud." The wavering mists were seen only over relatively new graves.

The very old ones showed no manifestation at all. This further confirms Reichenbach's idea. It is not impossible that this phenomenon gave rise to the folk/occult idea that dead spirits hang around for three days before moving on.

### Summary of Reichenbach's Findings

Only the highlights of Reichenbach's work have been given here. For lack of space, no mention has been made of his work with heat, electricity and stars and planets other than the sun and moon. To conclude this chapter, I quote just a few of his conclusions as to the nature of od, conclusions which have a bearing on later chapters:

- *"Magnet flames and their light exhibit such complete resemblance to the aura, that I believe myself compelled to consider the two as identical."*

- *"Every crystal, natural or artificial, exercises a specific exciting power on the animal nerves, weak in the healthy, strong in the diseased."*

- *"[The force] does not attract iron, does not cause any freely moving body to assume directions referable to the terrestrial poles, does not affect the magnet, does not induce a galvanic current in wires, and consequently it is not a magnetism."*

- *"It may be charged and transferred upon other bodies by mere contact."*

- *"Matter has a power of conducting it, in different degrees, in proportion to the continuity of bodies."*

- *"The capacity of bodies to receive a charge is in direct relation to the strength of the . . . force."*

- *"The [earth's magnetic field] exercises in sensitive persons, healthy and sick, a peculiar exciting action, strong enough to interfere with their rest, in the healthy, to modify their sleep; in the sick, to disturb the circulation of the blood, the function of the nerves, and the equilibrium of the vital force."*

- *"Magnetized water . . . is altered water."*

- *"The force of the human hand may be conducted through other bodies, exactly like the crystallic force, and these bodies are capable of conducting the two forces in the same way."*

- *"The force of the hands possess the same capability of accumulation as the crystallic force."*

- *"The action of the sun agrees with those of crystals, the magnets, and the human hand."*

- *"The greatest influence in reference to a force corresponding to that of crystals is manifested in the outer borders of the red and violet-blue rays of the solar spectrum."*

- *"The light of the moon possesses the force now under consideration in a strong degree."*

- *"The transfer of the . . . force from one body to another is effected without contact by the mere approximation of them toward each other."*

- *"This force not only manifests itself in contact, but also at distances, as from the sun, moon and stars; so, also, from all matter."*

- *"The effective force . . . does not appertain to particular forms or especial qualities of matter, but it dwells in matter in and by itself."*

- *"It is all-pervasive, without a known insulator, and extends over the entire universe."*

To Baron Charles von Reichenbach we owe a tremendous debt for his bravery in plunging into an area of research so derided by his colleagues, and for meticulously recording his experiments so that we may be saved many years of effort. His researches provide invaluable material with which to compare the work of later experimenters. In the history of *vril* physics, by whatever name it may eventually be called, Reichenbach will stand out as one of the giant contributors to our knowledge.

# 4
# Wilhelm Reich and Orgone Energy

I have praised Mesmer and von Reichenbach as giants in the field of *vril* physics. The next man whose work will be discussed was a genius as well as a giant. Brilliant, eccentric, versatile, egotistical, inventive, ambitious, humanitarian, antagonistic—Wilhelm Reich was all of these and much more. He was a man seemingly born too late and too soon. In an age of specialization he appeared like a throwback to the multidisciplined generalists of two hundred years ago, crisscrossing and delving into nearly every field of science. In an age of mundane details and statistical research, he was futuristic in developing a means of controlling the climate of the world, establishing the basis for a new social order, and working on ways to use the energy of the cosmos for intergalactic travel. Highly criticized for not sufficiently documenting and proving his findings to the satisfaction of the scientific establishment, he often said that his role was to blaze trails to new knowledge; it was the role of others to cultivate what he discovered.

Reich's controversial career really began in 1919 in medical school when he joined a group of radicals led by a man named Sigmund Freud. He worked his way quickly into a position of leadership (he was only twenty-two when he joined the group) and wrote several well-accepted articles and books on psychoanalysis. But already his brilliance carried him beyond, and isolated him from, his contemporaries. By 1935 his social theories and his extension of Freud's ideas in a direction Freud did not want to go had gotten him dismissed from the International Psychoanalytic Association in Austria and Germany. He withdrew to Norway and set up a clinic and laboratory, where he made the discoveries that were to launch him into the most important phase of his life. But he succeeded in antagonizing the scientific community there, and within three years he set sail for the United States. Here he carried on an immense variety of experiments and vainly tried to interest Albert Einstein and other scientists in his work. His unorthodox methods, antagonizing manner and, in the light of contemporary knowledge, fantastic claims for his discoveries alienated him from the American medical and scientific community until, in 1954, he was accused of various malpractices by the FDA. Significantly, he was never convicted on any of the charges, but was eventually sentenced to prison for contempt when he refused to enter the court for trial. Nevertheless, according to official records, the FDA felt it necessary to confiscate, ban and burn all his books, even those having nothing to do with the case. Reich died in 1957, shortly before he was to be released from prison. He was a martyr, but largely of his own making.

### Another Name for *Vril*

"Orgone," also called "orgone energy" and "OR," is the name Reich gave to the energy he worked with. It is derived from the words "organic" and "orgasm."

Like od, it is easily formed into new words, such as "orgonometric," "orgonotic," "orgonomic." Reich made his discoveries through quite a different route from other researchers. Studying under Freud, he became convinced that libido is an actual energy in the body and not merely a concept, as Freud and his followers later came to view it. He made intensive clinical studies of the orgasm, eventually seeing it as an electric-like discharge of energy that followed a four-beat pattern: mechanical tension, charge, discharge, relaxation. In a truly healthy person, he surmised the discharge should be accompanied by convulsive, involuntary movements of the body, and the relaxation stage should be accompanied by a warm, spreading glow as the released energy reached every part of the body.

Where there was no involuntary convulsing nor any glow sensation, which was what Reich found in the majority of the cases he studied, he reasoned that there was subconscious blocking of the energy flow caused by neurotic complexes. That such complexes block the flow of body energy is also an ancient Hawaiian idea. Further, Reich maintained that a chronic blockage of the OR energy could cause disease, another ancient concept. This led him to the discovery of seven transverse muscle segments commonly found in a state of chronic tension in neurotic patients. One circled the head at the level of the forehead and eyes; the next was the area around the mouth and jaw; then around the throat; the chest; the solar plexus or diaphragm; the abdomen; and finally the pelvis. Note the correspondence to the yoga system of chakras through which kundalini passes. Originally Reich described these groupings in a different, random order, but I have rearranged them to show the correspondence. It is not known whether Reich studied yoga, but in view of his many interests it would not be surprising if he had.

Therefore he may have mixed up the order in describing them so that the correlation would not be too obvious to his colleagues. Reich found that when these chronic muscle spasms were released through exercise and massage, there would first be an emotional release, and then the patient would feel "streamings" of energy through the body. Very often physical ailments would clear up shortly thereafter.

In Norway, Reich made the first of the discoveries that were to lead him to the practical utilization of what he called "atmospheric orgone." In one experiment some ocean sand heated to incandescence continued to glow with a blue color. Subjects felt this radiation as a prickling on the skin, but it did not have the same characteristics as other known forms of radiation. If allowed to touch the skin, it produced a reddening within a few minutes, and the spot later grew inflamed and painful. After many experiments, Reich postulated that the heating released the orgone absorbed by the sand from the rays of the sun. The intense amount of orgone released caused the air in his laboratory to feel "heavy," and people in the room developed headaches within half an hour. Reich also mentioned that all metal objects in the room became highly magnetized. We have to assume he meant only iron and steel ones, since he did not specify. This is an extremely significant discovery if true, but unfortunately, neither I nor anyone I know of has duplicated this finding. It may simply be that our energy concentrations have not been high enough yet.

Trying to photograph the radiation, Reich found that every photographic plate in the room became fogged, even the ones he used as controls. This led him to the conclusion that the energy is present everywhere, the same conclusion reached by Reichenbach and Mesmer. Attempting to determine more visual effects, Reich

observed the sand cultures in a dark basement for
hours at a time. The results are very reminiscent of
Reichenbach's:

> *After the eyes had become adapted to the darkness,
> the room did not appear black, but* gray-blue. *There
> were fog-like formations and bluish dots and lines
> of light. Violet light phenomena seemed to emanate
> from the walls as well as from various objects in
> the room. When I held a magnifying glass before
> my eyes, these light impressions, all of them blue
> or gray-blue,* became more intense.

Reichenbach would have called him a good sensitive.
Other effects Reich noted were that he apparently
developed conjunctivitis after remaining in the room
with the sand cultures for several hours, and over a
period of time he developed an overall tan without
having been in the sun.

With high concentrations of *vril,* induced either
organically or mechanically, a number of my laboratory
subjects have noted the bluish-gray fog-like formations
as well as the dots and lines of light. In their eyes, the
"fog" actually bears more of a resemblance to so-called
heat waves. Violet light emanating from a *vril* generator
has been observed, though rarely, and on two occasions
a condition similar to conjunctivitis appeared. However, it is possible this was due to simple eyestrain. No
tanning has been noted, but our energy concentration
may not have been high enough.

## Conductors and Nonconductors

Reich also found that insulating materials, noncon-
ductors, could be charged with orgone if they were left
in the sun for a length of time, and that high humidity,
ventilation in the shade or immersion in water could

discharge them. Up to now he was repeating much of what Reichenbach discovered, even to living subjects charging objects. The first "law" he formulated in regard to atmospheric orgone is that "organic substances absorb the orgone energy and retain it."

Seeking to confine orgone in an enclosed space to study it, Reich made both a fundamental error of fact and a tremendous discovery. Experience with sand cultures seemed to indicate that a metal box would contain the orgone energy within it. Reich thought this occurred by reflection and guessed that if the metal reflected orgone inward it would also reflect it outward, probably because he felt it would act as a conductor. To counteract this, he conceived the idea of covering the outside of the metal box with a layer of organic material to absorb the reflected orgone. To his astonishment, the box gave off the same blue visual effects whether or not the sand culture was in it, and this in spite of taking the box apart and immersing it in water to discharge the orgone. Every time he put organic material back on the box, the orgone effects showed up, and every time he constructed an identical box which had never been in contact with the sand culture, it still showed up. To explain this, Reich formulated the idea that the energy had to come from the atmosphere itself. The following statement, which Reich calls an insight of far-reaching importance, demonstrates his intuitive reasoning which so irked his enemies and dismayed his colleagues: *"The energy which governs the living is of necessity identical with the atmospheric energy;* otherwise, it would not have led to the discovery of the atmospheric energy."

The tremendous discovery made by Reich was that by increasing the number of layers of metallic and organic material (each such combination came to be known as a "fold") he could increase the intensity of the energy inside the box. The fundamental error was in his explanation of how this intensification came into being. He believed that metals absorbed orgone rapidly and expelled it rapidly, while organic materials absorbed it slowly and expelled it slowly. Thus, an organic layer on the outside of a box would absorb energy from the atmosphere and pass it on to the adjacent metal layer, which would immediately pass it on to the next organic layer, and so on. So much orgone would be absorbed by the organic layers that by the time it got to the inside of the box it would be amplified.

My own research shows this view to be incorrect, even though many questions in regard to my findings remain unanswered. The events leading to my discovery are important. In 1972 I was experimenting with a pyramid designed to sharpen razor blades (pyramids are fully discussed in Chapter 5) by means of an unknown energy. At the same time I was doing some writing on sexology and ran across the works of Reich. What first intrigued me was a dehydration effect reported both by pyramid researchers and by Reich during experiments with intense orgone concentrations. Reich also noted that plastic seemed to be a good absorber of orgone. This stimulated me to remember a razor blade that remained sharp for an unusually long time while I kept it in a plastic soap dish. Wondering whether I had inadvertently been using orgone and whether it might be the same as the pyramid energy, I embarked on a series of experiments which proved rather conclusively that they were the same, at least by the Law of the Elephant (remember, if it looks like an elephant, etc.).

First, I merely kept a Gillette Platinum Plus blade in the plastic box between shaves. After two hundred smooth shaves I decided to experiment on a more serious basis. Nowhere in Reich's available works is there any indication that he ever used his layered box, first called an "orgone accumulator" and later shortened to "orac," for sharpening anything. Nevertheless, I converted the plastic box into a one-fold orac by lining it with aluminum foil. Using a Gillette Blue Blade, usually good for only five or six shaves, I began keeping a careful record of results. Twenty-nine shaves later the blade refused to sharpen anymore. Recalling that orientation is important to the effects in a pyramid, I lined up the short ends of my little box in a north-south direction with the edges of the blade of the razor facing the same directions. This worked for a few days, and then the blade became rough again. So I reoriented the blade with the edges facing east and west. The blade sharpened once more.

The next step was an important one with implications that are still being studied. Keeping the blade aligned to magnetic north, I moved the box itself out of alignment. There was no change; the blade continued to sharpen. It was obvious that there was some kind of energy operating inside the box, because the blade would not sharpen outside of it. It was equally obvious that the energy was interacting with the magnetic field of the earth to sharpen the blade. So far, this is the only type of orac experiment I know of in which orientation is a necessary factor. Reich never mentioned orientation as a factor, and, in our other orac experiments it does not seem to make any difference.

### Oracs and Manaboxes

My investigations led to the development of the Manabox, a small, copper-lined plastic box 3"x3"x½", which might be described as a modified one-fold orac. It differs from an orac in that nothing is placed inside the box. I have found through hundreds of experiments that energy effects pass right through the plastic cover. A razor blade can be sharpened by merely aligning it properly and laying it on top of the cover. Twenty-five to fifty shaves with a Blue Blade are common, and over one hundred shaves have been reported. When the Manabox was first developed, I was still thinking in terms of Reich's absorption concept, but a chance remark by my seven-year-old son changed my thinking and opened up a whole new area of investigation. It also led to the discovery of Reich's fundamental error.

The base of the Manabox is lined with copper, but not the cover, because I was following Reich's thesis that a metal-lined box would concentrate the energy toward the interior. At first I thought that the effects on top of the box were some kind of spillover phenomenon. The remark of my son was that, to him, the energy felt stronger on the *bottom* of the box, where the copper was laying flat. I quickly tested this idea with a number of people familiar with the effects of *vril.* I had them hold the box in various positions over sensitive areas of the skin, like the palm of the hand and the forehead. Everyone reported the same subjective sensation.

After repeated experimentation with *objective* results, such as sharpening of blades, dehydration of foods and

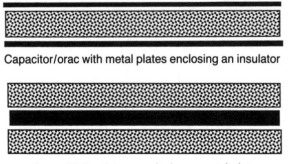

Capacitor/orac with metal plates enclosing an insulator

Orac with insulators enclosing a metal plate

stimulation of plant growth, with subjects totally un-
familiar with *vril*, I came to the inescapable conclusion
that an energy *field* is created whenever a metallic and
nonmetallic layer are joined together. This is true
whether the materials are in the form of a box or
simply flat plates, and regardless of which material is
uppermost. The more the layers, the more intense the
field. This field is created the instant the two materials
are joined together.

The new field is apparently globular in form, that is,
it extends all around the two pieces of joined materials,
and does not appear to be significantly stronger on one
side or the other. Therefore, the effect Reich was
obtaining in his enclosed orac appears not to be due
to an absorption process, but to the intensification
produced by the intersecting fields of several plates.
Many new devices have emerged out of this research,
such as the Manaplate, a sheet of metal between two
sheets of plastic, and the Manabloc, a sheet of metal
immersed in resin. Both produce all the effects of
oracs, Manaboxes and pyramids.

### Creating Fields

Now, joining metals and nonmetals to create a field
reminds one of the voltaic battery. This is a setup
whereby different metals are alternated in layers
separated by an electrolyte (a solution capable of
conducting electricity). Sometimes they are separated
by organic matter soaked in an electrolyte. This
generates an electric current. However, if the
electrolyte dries up, the battery will no longer work.
The relationship between this and the orac seems
slight.

Much more intriguing is the capacitor or condenser.
This is a device that accumulates an electric charge
and holds it until it is discharged through an outside

agent. A capacitor is constructed with two pieces of metal separated by an insulator. When direct current is run into it, an electrical field is built up between the two pieces of metal until the limit of the capacitor's absorption capacity is reached. Then no more current can flow until it has discharged. The similarity in construction to an orac or Manaplate is very interesting. A sensative person can feel *vril* effects from a commercial capacitor, indicating that a capacitor is generating *vril* or orgone merely by means of its construction. And a large enough orac or Manaplate will act as a natural capacitor, gradually drawing an electrical charge from the atmosphere.

Placing capacitors in series increases their capacitance, that is, their ability to absorb electricity. This is equivalent to increasing the number of folds in an orac. Furthermore, the use of different kinds of insulators alters the ability of a capacitor to hold a charge as some materials can hold more of a charge than others. I have found that different insulators alter the intensity of a field in an orac or similar device, and so far the effects of insulators used in oracs and capacitors correlate strongly. Different metals change the conductivity in capacitors and, apparently, the quality of the field in oracs.

Finally, capacitance increases in a capacitor according to the increase in size of the plate area. Experiments not fully verified tend toward the conclusion that an increase in fold area also increases the orgone field intensity. Surely, here is a rich area of research for the electronically minded.

### Effects of Different Metals

I spoke of a qualitative difference with different metals, and I will elaborate. Reich preferred to use steel in his oracs, either galvanized sheets, mesh or steel wool. He never fully explained why, other than saying it had a better effect on the human body. He barely mentioned copper, but he described aluminum as dangerous to the organism. This latter claim was based on an experiment he performed in which cancerous mice treated with an aluminum-lined orac died faster than others. I have found only one reference to one such experiment in his writings. In hundreds of tests with aluminum-lined oracs, some lasting many years, I have had nothing but beneficial effects. While not yet drawing definite conclusions, I suspect the demise of the mice was caused by something other than the aluminum itself.

In tests, I have had subjects "charge" themselves by placing one hand on a Manaplate for one minute or less. With a copper-lined generator the usual result is increased alertness and energy. With aluminum, one usually experiences a feeling of soothing calm and relaxation. Iron and steel are somewhere in between activating and calming. This middle position may be why Reich preferred these metals for his therapeutic work. With either copper or aluminum there may be subjective sensations of prickling, coolness, warmth, tingling, etc., but these vary greatly with the subject and the time of day. The activating and calming effects are much more regular, though, as Reich found, people differ in their ability to absorb the energy and in their reactions to it. For instance, while most people report an activating influence from copper, a few subjects say copper calms and relaxes them.

Put under the pillow at night, a copper-lined Mana-bloc either initiates or relieves insomnia, according to reports, depending on the individual. In the majority of cases it induces vivid dreams, at least during the first few nights of use. As a tolerance to the energy builds up, the effects become less dramatic, just as reported by Reich.

One case is indicative of the general rule with copper and aluminum. A researcher took a 3x (x = fold) copper-lined Manaplate to bed and put it under his pillow. His wife was already in a sound sleep. In a short time she awoke and stayed awake, while he was able to doze only lightly. Neither could go back to sleep until the plate was moved away from the bed. The next night, unknown to his wife, he placed an aluminum-lined Manaplate under the pillow. They both fell asleep as soon as they lay down and slept soundly all night.

## Healing Power

Reich was intensely concerned with the medical bene-fits of orgone. He was also intensely concerned with possible dangers arising from its use. He took pains to emphasize that no one should use an orac with more than three layers for medical purposes without medical supervision. Nonetheless, he said:

> *Orgone irradiation can be applied with great benefit and without any danger, even with over-irradiation, in the following diseases:* Fatigue, anemia, cancer biopathy, *with the exception of tumors of the brain and liver,* acute and chronic colds, hay fever, rheumatism, arthritis, chronic ulcers, *any kind of lesion, abrasion, wounds, burns, sinusitis, and some types of migraine.*

Neuroses cannot be cured by orgone, he declared, only some of its symptoms alleviated.

I do not have a background in medicine and therefore am not competent to judge medical matters related to orgone. However, I can cite specific

incidents that seem to have a bearing on what Reich
claimed. For one thing, fatigue has been relieved
hundreds of times by researchers and subjects putting a
hand on a *vril* generator. To be more accurate, let me
say that the person felt energetic after being charged.
In just as many cases, pain from minor cuts, bruises,
aches from muscles and headaches have been alleviated
in seconds after contact with, generally, a 1x generator,
such as the Manabox. Sinus passages have also cleared
after a short period of contact. Colds are a rarity
among those who frequent my home, where I store
many *vril* generators, and some people have reported
relief from symptoms of arthritis after regular contact
with a Manabox. I am not prepared to say how much
of this is due to suggestion or other causes and how
much to orgone or *vril*.

An experience I had illustrates the healing power of
*vril*. I was carving a roast for dinner when the knife
slipped and struck my left forefinger quite hard,
between the nail and the first joint. It felt as though it
hit bone. Blood shot for several feet until a napkin
was applied as a pressure bandage. The cut was
curved and about a half an inch long. I immediately
held a 3x Manabloc under the cut finger. Within
minutes all pain subsided. Within an hour the napkin
was removed. The edges of the wound had sealed
together and one tiny part looked as if it had healed
over. My wife, who has some medical experience, had
expected that several stitches would be required. She
was amazed when she saw what had happened. I
refused to apply a bandage, as I wanted to see how
healing would progress. I took a shower and went out
for the evening, without any problem from the finger.
The next day I showed it to several people who thought
it was either a surface scratch or a cut that had been
healing for two weeks or more. No ordinary scab ever

formed on this cut and no antiseptics were applied.
(Please note that I am not recommending that anyone
try this. I am merely reporting what happened.)

## Boxes and Tubes

Reich mainly used two types of oracs in his work. One
was a box designed to put things inside. It might range
in size from slightly larger than the Manabox to large
enough for a person to sit in. The other type was called
a "shooter." Its purpose was to conduct a high concentration of orgone to a particular place, such as a
specific area of the body. The simplest type was a glass
test tube lightly stuffed with steel wool. This was often
used for problems like minor cuts and treating the
gums. The open end was directed toward the area
to be treated, in line with the metal-reflection theory.
Another type of shooter consisted of an enclosed,
layered box, from which extended a flexible iron tube
(BX cable) with a funnel on the end. The orgone was to
flow from the box through the tube and be spread out
by the funnel shape. My question is whether the orgone
flowed through the space in the tube or through the
metal walls. Reichenbach found that material objects
such as wire, thread or string, when attached to a concentrated source conduct energy. I have demonstrated
the same thing. Based on these experiments, I strongly
suspect that energy was flowing through material, not
space, in Reich's shooter. I have not tried it yet, but it
is possible that plastic tubing would work just as well
as BX cable. It remains to be seen whether metal or
nonmetal is the better conductor of the energy, if either
of them is.

For those who may be considering building an orac, I
should clear up some possible confusion in terminology. When Reich spoke of a threefold orac, he meant a

box with six sides, each side with three layers, each
layer consisting of one sheet of metal and one sheet of
nonmetal. My 3x Manaplate is the equivalent of only
one side of a Reichian threefold orac. In my terms,
then, Reich had concentrated an 18x force inside his
orac (six 3x sides).

## Charging Water

One of Reich's early findings was that water is one of
the best absorbers of orgone. This, of course, was nothing new. Mesmer and Reichenbach before him had
discovered it. So had spiritual healers and religious
leaders all over the world. But Reich did prove it in a
more scientific way than anyone before him. It is odd,
though, that he apparently did not consider the value of
giving charged water to patients as others had.

One observation he made was that water with "high
orgonotic potency," that is, highly charged with
orgone, tastes sweet. My own experiments confirm this.
I left a glass container of tap water with a noticeable
chlorine taste on a *vril* generator for periods varying
from five minutes to half an hour. I performed double-
blind experiments, with subjects tasting a control
sample of tap water drawn at the same time as the
water to be treated. Nearly all the fifty-odd subjects
agreed that there was a difference between the treated
water and the fresh tap water, and most preferred the
treated water. Some said it tasted sweetish; others said
it was smooth, like fresh spring water; still others said
it tasted flat. The most generally agreed-upon reaction
was that the taste was "smoothed out." I tried the
experiment with coffee, wine, cider and carbonated
beverages. Bitterness, tartness, chemical taste and car-
bonation appeared greatly reduced or eliminated altogether. It is amazing how quickly cheap wine and
brandy can become smoothly aged!

Some people could taste a difference after five minutes. For others it took longer. Some of my new generators produce dramatic taste changes in about thirty seconds. In 1948 Reich stated: "It has not yet been possible to conduct an exact biochemical analysis, but one is planned." Whether or not the water is changed biochemically, it is an excellent conductor of electricity, and glass is a good insulator. A glass of water, then, is a natural capacitor and potential *vril* generator, and like any capacitor can be charged with energy.

Another experiment with water led to a new discovery. In an attempt to reduce discoloration of the water, I taped a Manabox to the side of a seventeen-gallon aquarium inhabited by four fish. In a few days the water was crystal clear, but that was not the most important result. To my surprise, the algae disappeared, and there was no more growth of algae in the tank. Numerous experiments confirmed that orgone/*vril* in high enough concentrations prevents the growth of algae while promoting the health of the fish. Conditions that affected algae growth were the amount and the source of light permitted to enter the tank, the size of the tank, and whether or not fresh, untreated water was added. With untreated water an "explosion" of algae occurred in the tank within twenty-four to forty-eight hours. Within a week, however, if the energy concentration was high enough, the algae again was greatly reduced or eliminated.

I do not know why algae, which are one-cell or multi-cell plants, are so affected unless the energy concentration is too high for them to sustain. A Manabox will kill a small plant if left next to it continuously. However, if the energy is given in small doses, or if water is used as the medium for transferring the energy from the box to the plant, effects are beneficial. Interestingly, the death of the plants resembles the death of plants and trees noted by Reich when they were affected by "DOR" (deadly orgone). In both cases, plants died from the tops downward. DOR, according to Reich, was a condition in which naturally free-flowing orgone became static and heavily concentrated, and in the process became dangerous to humans, animals and plants. One way in which the DOR condition started was by contact between a concentration of orgone and a source of radioactivity. Reich noted a dehydration effect when this happened, so he assumed that drought and desert conditions are caused by the existence of a "cloud" of DOR. This led him into another astounding phase of work.

## Cloudbusting

An invisible cloud of DOR had settled over Reich's headquarters in Rangeley, Maine, as a result of an experiment gone awry. He wanted to dissipate this. He recalled an early experience in which a tube directed at the waves on a lake seemed to affect their motion. In his intuitive way, he made a leap from this observation to the construction of an elaborate "Cloudbuster." The Cloudbuster was a collection of telescoping metal pipes mounted on the bed of a truck. One end of the pipes was pointed toward the sky like antiaircraft guns, and the other end was attached to BX cables leading to a nearby body of water. This device apparently had the power to dissipate or form clouds and to cause air movement. The principle was based on the assumption that the tubes had the effect of "drawing" orgone from the place at which they were aimed. While pointing at a cloud, they would draw the orgone from it, thereby reducing its potential and its ability to hold together. So it would dissipate. Pointing the pipes at a clear area of the sky would cause nearby clouds to grow, or, if carried out long enough, new clouds to form.

Reich's explanation of why this took place is not clear, but the records of his experiments are impressive. He apparently brought rain to drought-stricken Maine and was thanked for it in the press. He may have inadvertently caused storms over Boston and New York. He realized what a dangerous thing he was working with and repeatedly emphasized caution in attempting to control the weather. Various attempts to repeat his weather experiments have had mixed results. Reich was looking toward the day when deserts could be made to bloom like healthy orgonotic entities, and vast new areas would be opened up for food production.

Reich had his troubles with the Cloudbuster. It did not always operate according to theory, and the same trouble has besieged his followers. However, I once attended an orgone energy conference in Toronto, Canada, where one participant had brought his homemade Cloudbuster. Early one morning when the sky was clear and clear weather had been forecast for several days ahead, he pointed his contraption at the horizon and left it there. By late afternoon clouds were forming along the horizon. By evening the sky was overcast, and the next day it rained. Weather can be unpredictable, so this does not constitute proof that the Cloudbuster was responsible for this change, but the possibility is intriguing.

I have just begun some research along this line. It is too early for definite conclusions, but I have indications that tubes do affect the flow of orgone. Specifically, a reasonably sensitive person can feel a cool-breeze effect when holding a hand near the end of a tube, any kind of tube. In experiments, blindfolded subjects were able to tell when their hand passed over

the end of a stationary tube. The sensation reported
varied between that of a very slight cool breeze and
that of a pulling, like magnetic attraction. If these
effects reflect an objective condition, it seems to partly
substantiate Reich's thesis that a tube draws orgone.
My tube was not the four-meter length that Reich said
was necessary for a Cloudbuster to operate properly.
But *vril* effects have been experienced from tubes that
range from three-inch plastic pipes to metal and plastic
cigar tubes. Like Reich, I have found that several tubes
bound together produce a stronger effect.

## The Orgone Motor

Students of energy are most intrigued by Reich's work
on developing orgone into a motive force for powering
engines and electrical generators. In 1947, experiments
with Geiger counters and oracs led Reich to believe
that this was possible. He believed locomotion in living
organisms comes from the motive force of orgone. By
1948, with five witnesses present, Reich is said to have
set a motor in motion by means of an orac and vacuum
tubes that had been "soaked" in orgone for a certain
period of time. Another ingredient, called "Y" in the
report that Reich made, may have been an electric battery, according to W. E. Mann in *Orgone, Reich and
Eros.* It is not known what part the battery played in
the setup. A. S. Neill, a close friend of Reich's, said that
as far as he knew the motor idea was never followed
up. Jerome Eden, an ardent follower of Reich, claimed
that two "orgone motors" were stolen from Reich and
delivered behind the Iron Curtain. In 1956, in a court
appeal, Reich himself briefly mentioned the 1948
experiment and went on to say that it was the first step
"in the technological development toward noiseless,
smokeless, smooth-functioning locomotor machines of
the future." His statements are unclear as to whether

an actual orgone motor was developed or whether the
1948 experiment was the only one of its kind. However, if orgone ran a motor once, it can be done again.
Very probably, the solution is in developing a means to
convert orgone energy into electrical energy, and not in
trying to use orgone directly.

I have made a small, but significant step toward this
goal in my laboratory. I have proven without a doubt
that even small amounts of orgone can induce a charge
in an ordinary flashlight battery. In an experiment in
1972 I purchased four size C batteries and tested them
with Sanwa model U-50 DNC Multimeter using a #44
lamp load. All four produced 1.55 volts. I numbered
them 1 through 4. They were then shorted to the
following voltages:

#1 - .2V

#2 - .1V

#3 - .3V

#4 - .2V

The batteries were left standing overnight, and I tested
them again the next morning the same way. They were
then distributed as follows: #1 was placed on a 40x
aluminum/plastic Manabox; #2 on a 1x copper/plastic
Manabox; #3 in a six-inch styrene pyramid; and #4 was
used as a control. All batteries were checked daily at
9:30 A.M. for one week and at the same hour at weekly
intervals for two weeks. On the last day they were
taken off the test arrangements and checked again
twenty-four hours later. Here are the results:

Day 1 (before the test): #1 - .95V

#2 - .9V

#3 - .95V

#4 - .95V

NOTE: It is usual for discharged batteries to regain
some charge from just standing around, probably

because their capacitor-like construction absorbs
ambient (surrounding) energy.

| Day 2 | all batteries 1V |
|-------|------------------|
| Day 3 | #1 - 1.05V |
|       | #2 - 1V |
|       | #3 - 1.05V |
|       | #4 - 1V |

Notice that #1 and #3 have moved ahead of the
control, #4, and that #2, which had been discharged the
most originally, is nevertheless equal to the control.

| Day 4 | #1 - 1.09V |
|-------|------------|
|       | #2 - 1.01V |
|       | #3 - 1.05V |
|       | #4 - 1.01V |

All have increased except #3.

| Day 5 | #1 - 1.1V |
|-------|-----------|
|       | #2 - 1.05V |
|       | #3 - 1.1V |
|       | #4 - 1.05V |

All have increased and #3 has caught up with #1.

| Day 6 | no change |
|-------|-----------|
| Day 7 | #1 - 1.15V |
|       | #2 - 1.09V |
|       | #3 - 1.1V |
|       | #4 - 1.05V |

The control and #3 have not changed for three days,
while #1 and #2 have both increased even more.

| Day 14 | #1 - 1.1V |
|--------|-----------|
|        | #2 - 1.09V |
|        | #3 - 1.09V |
|        | #4 - 1.05V |

One week later the only change is that #1 and #3 have dropped slightly.

Day 22    #1 - 1.2V
#2 - 1.19V
#3 - .9V (???)
#4 - 1.1V

Day 23    no change

Although the amounts are small, it is clear that the test batteries definitely increased in voltage over the control during the first week. Even #2, which started out with .05V less than the others, climbed up past the control by the seventh day. #1 had the most marked change, which suggests that the greater number of layers in that Manabox were probably a factor. The drop of .05V in #1 in the second week is puzzling, as is the subsequent jump of .1V during the next week. So is the jump of .1V in #2 in the same week. Note that #4 also increased by .05 in that week after remaining steady at 1.05 for a week and a half. Relatively startling is the sudden drop in #3, which was in the pyramid, to a point below all the rest after climbing steadily.

Obviously some environmental factor interacted with the batteries that week. It might have been sunspots, although radio reception seemed normal. The only other environmental changes that I could discover at the time—and I'm not saying that they were factors— were that Venus went direct on day 15 and Mercury went retrograde on day 17. At any rate, it seems strongly evident that an orgone/capacitor type of device can amplify the conversion of ambient energy into usable electrical power. It would be useful for others to repeat the experiment to determine if there is any consistency in the results and also to include a battery that is held in the hand and willfully charged.

## Summary

Reich leaped headlong into so many areas that it is very hard to follow his work. His immediate followers who have remained with the work have stuck close to the medical aspects of "Orgonomy," as he called his new science. Only now, as interest in new energy sources is being sparked, are people beginning to take an unprejudiced look at the far-reaching implications of Reich's work. His theoretical bases may not turn out to be wholly correct, but there is ample evidence that orgone exists and performs work.

There are several simple ways to experiment with Reich's concepts. One is to purchase or make an "orgone blanket." Originally, this was made of two or more wool blankets with the edges sewn together and the spaces in between filled with steel wool padding. I believe there are still a few people who manufacture this. Reich used it to cover patients, with the idea that the field generated by the layers would help release muscle blocks and promote healing. But many more recent users report that it gives them a sense of well-being and increased energy even when there is no illness.

A simpler and very effective version is the so-called "space blanket," used for maintaining body warmth in cold weather. It also produces the orgone effects, apparently because of its layered plastic and aluminum construction. For general experimentation, it is hard to beat layers of plain old aluminum foil between layers of quality plastic wrap, as many layers as desired, in whatever shape is most appropriate for the experiment one has in mind.

Reich's work has such potential that all dedicated *vril* researchers need to study the research of this controversial genius.

# 5
# The Power Behind Pyramidology

In the very distant past of our planet—some say forty-five hundred years ago, some say fifty thousand, some say long before that—someone or some group designed a totally unique structure. Why they designed it is still the subject of debate. Where they got the knowledge to design it as they did is not certain. What is certain is that it was designed and built and remains standing today, a giant memory of the past—the Great Pyramid of Egypt.

Stories of the origin of the Great Pyramid vary greatly. Among archeologists specializing in Egyptian archeology, the common view is that it was built as a tomb for the pharaoh Khufu, or Cheops, as he is more generally known. This view is primarily based on the finding of hieroglyphs resembling his seal on stones inside the pyramid. Despite overwhelming evidence that the Great Pyramid was anything but a tomb, including the fact that a body was never found inside its well-sealed chambers, Egyptologists persist in their theory, generating a story of tens of thousands of slaves put to work over decades building a mountain of stone in which to put the corpse of one man. Curiously, the meticulous record-keepers of ancient Egypt did not leave one word or hieroglyph about the pyramid. Also, the earliest image known—a fresco of slaves being forced to haul blocks of stone on wood sledges—was painted one thousand years after the date many Egyptologists believe the pyramid was constructed.

A more esoteric theory has it that the Great Pyramid was built by Atlanteans as a storehouse of knowledge intended to survive the Flood. Certainly, the technology represented in the construction of the pyramid is far more advanced than what is usually attributed to the Egyptians of five thousand years ago. Another esoteric theory is that the pyramid was a temple of initiation, suggested by certain references in *The Egyptian Book of the Dead.* Perhaps the most incredible theory is that the Great Pyramid was built by highly intelligent beings from outer space as a kind of beacon or landmark.

The Great Pyramid could have been used for so many different things, and probably was at various times, that it boggles the mind to think that human beings could have projected such a vast array of data and potentials into a single structure. It has been shown that the pyramid was an accurate almanac by which the length of the year and its fraction of .2422 could be calculated with as much ease as with a modern telescope. It serves as a surveyor's instrument, a theodolite of great precision, as well as a finely oriented compass. It could have been used as a geodetic landmark for the construction of structures in the ancient world. It was a celestial observatory and a scale model of the hemisphere, correctly incorporating degrees of latitude and longitude, from which highly accurate maps of the northern hemisphere could be drawn. It probably was the model for a system of weights and measures based on the polar axis of rotation.

Another possible use was to provide water to the

area. One ingenious gentleman has shown how the
pyramid could have been used as a pump to draw
water from the Nile, while another has shown how the
original limestone covering could have condensed
water out of the desert air.

What a marvel of marvels! Yet the fact that the
pyramid *could* have been used for all those things does
not necessarily mean that it was. After all, an automobile, in addition to its use as a motor vehicle, can
serve as a house, an office, a chicken coop, a battering
ram, an initiation chamber and a casket. But did its
makers have those things in mind when they built it?

The Great Pyramid is a huge structure, some 481
feet high and covering an area of more than 13 acres.
One side almost faces true north, with an accuracy
difficult even for modern building engineers. Its
structure incorporates in a number of unmistakable
ways the mathematical concept of pi (3.1416...), even
though Egyptologists say that number was not in use
until a thousand years later. Pi's appearance in the
pyramid they attribute to chance. The angle of the sides
to the base is 51 degrees 51 minutes 14 seconds, almost
identical to the face angle of a quartz crystal and to the
division of a circle into a seven-pointed star. Thus the
surface of each side does not make an equilateral triangle. Another mathematical relationship incorporated
in the structure of the pyramid—the one which will
interest us the most—is the relationship known as phi,
also called in Renaissance times "the golden section."
It is found in nature and is used in architecture to
produce pleasing forms. It represents the number 1.618,
which can be obtained by dividing a line at a point in
such a way that the ratio of the whole line to the larger
part is the same ratio as the larger part is to the
smaller. If we call the end points of the first whole line

A and C and the dividing point, B, then AC: AB = AB: BC = 1.618.

Now, you may ask, why are we playing mathematical games? For a very good reason. First, we should note what the ancients thought about phi. According to Egyptologist Schwaller de Lubicz, the Egyptians thought of phi as a symbol of creativity, the fire of life. Plato, in the Timaeus, called it the key to the physics of the cosmos. The Timaeus, by the way, is the work in which he described Atlantis. We might wonder why a number should receive such high praise. Granted, it is an important number, but enough to symbolize creativity, the "fire of life" or the key to physics? Let's take a look at another symbol, the word "pyramid" itself. It comes from the Greek and can be translated as "fire (pyr) in the middle." An odd name for a stone tomb, or even a stone observatory, theodolite, geodetic marker, pump or whatever. What kind of fire did the Greeks mean?

The first clue came in the 1930s when a Frenchman, André Bovis, was visiting the Great Pyramid and noticed that the corpses of some small animals found inside the pyramid were apparently mummified. That is, they were not decayed and did not smell. Back in France he experimented with models based on the dimensions of the Great Pyramid and gathered evidence that something about the shape caused the mummification of dead organic matter. In the 1940s in the United States, a dowser named Verne Cameron did more experiments with the pyramid shape and detected an energy field around it and energy streaming off the tips. He also found that if he linked the tips of several pyramids with wire or string in series or in parallel like batteries, the energy effect was amplified. In the 1950s Karl Drbal, a Czechoslovakian, discovered that

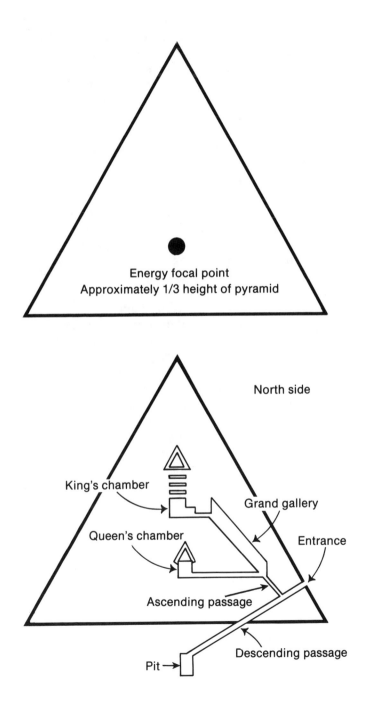

Energy focal point
Approximately 1/3 height of pyramid

North side

King's chamber

Grand gallery

Queen's chamber

Entrance

Ascending passage

Descending passage

Pit →

the same shape had a sharpening effect on razor blades and could also reduce or eliminate headaches. Gradually it was noticed that whatever energy was causing these phenomena seemed to be centered or focused at a point about one-third of the distance from the base to the apex, in the center of the pyramid, at about the same relative position of the King's Chamber in the original.

Considering the exactness of so many other measurements in the Great Pyramid, I was bothered by the vagueness of this focal point. Surely the Egyptians (or whoever designed it) must have known that the pyramid was also an energy generator. It was the Egyptian attitude toward phi along with Plato's comments that induced me to apply the phi relationship to the apex/base line in a pyramid. Using the formula described earlier, I found that in any pyramid constructed with the proportions of the Great Pyramid, the exact energy focal point is phi, or the dividing point on the line which produces the phi relationship. At that point there is the highest concentration of *vril,* the "fire of life" and the essence of creativity.

One of the most significant facts about the Great Pyramid and the models derived from it is that the most intensive energy effects are achieved when one side of the pyramid is facing magnetic north, which puts it in line with the electromagnetic field of the earth. As the orientation approaches 20 to 30 degrees away from north, the interior focus of energy virtually disappears. Magnetic north fluctuates, and it stands to reason that the Great Pyramid was oriented to get the greatest average energy effect while still achieving all of its other purposes. Researchers, including myself, have determined the intensity and focus of energy with dowsing devices and experiments with organic substances. Investigation of "pyramid energy" has been carried out ever since Bovis mummified his first dead cat. There are a great many aspects to it.

## Size, Shape and Substance

The Great Pyramid in Egypt, partly because of its size, is a powerful *vril* generator. When I visited the area in 1980 I found it hard to sleep in the adjacent town of Giza because of the energy, and of course the energy sensations inside the pyramid were considerable. However, similar energy effects can be obtained from models as small as four inches high, though the range of influence certainly is not as great. That means that the relationship between size and energy intensity is not a direct one; the intensity does not diminish in a regular way as you diminish the size of the model.

In the early days of pyramid experimentation, exact measurement was stressed, in the expectation that more precise measurements would result in greater energy effects. However, it did not turn out that way. In fact, there seems to be quite a bit of leeway in the shape and proportions of the models. In personal correspondence with Karl Drbal, I found that he and I agreed that an equilateral pyramid, with the base length equal to the corner lengths, worked just as well as one built to the proportions of the Cheops model (given at the end of the chapter). Even more surprising, the sides are not necessary. An early researcher decided to put small holes in the sides of his pyramids so that he could see experiments in progress. Another researcher wondered how big the holes could be without diminishing the pyramid effect. This led to the discovery that the mere frame of the pyramid—base lines and corners —worked as well as a pyramid with solid sides. In addition, tetrahedrons (often called three-sided pyramids) and cones work just as well.

The Great Pyramid is constructed primarily of limestone blocks. Since the experiments of Cameron and
Drbal, pyramid models have been made of cardboard,
concrete, wood, metal, plastic, cloth and anything else
people could think of. Aside from individual personal
preferences, the effects seem the same no matter what
the pyramid is made of.

## Organic Effects

An actual energy effect from the pyramid shape was
first noticed on dead animals. After years of experimentation, there is no doubt that energy concentrated
in a pyramid not only inhibits decay, but mummifies or
dehydrates dead organic matter. One time my loving
sons brought me a birthday present of a two-foot-long
dead shark they had found on the beach. They put it in
a four-foot high pyramid I had in the back yard. After a
couple of days the smell went away, sooner than you
might expect, and in two weeks the shark was
completely mummified.

Experiments with eggs, meat and fish show the average amount of dehydration to be 66 percent in relatively small pyramids. Greater dehydration seems to
occur with fruit and vegetables, probably because they
contain more water to begin with. Flowers become well
mummified without losing their petals or shape. In a
seventy-two-hour controlled experiment with apples,
I found no significant dehydration effect anywhere in a
six-inch high cardboard pyramid except at the phi
point. However, other experimenters have reported at
least some dehydration effects throughout the pyramid.

There has been considerable research with plants.
There are many reports of an increase in growth when
seeds are treated in a pyramid before planting, when
plants are grown in a pyramid, or when the water used

for plants is treated in a pyramid beforehand. I have consistently found that houseplants supplied with energized water grow faster and more abundantly than controls, their leaves are greener, and their roots fill up the pot faster. It has also been reported that crop yields increased up to two-and-a-half times the average when nourished with pyramid-treated water. One researcher reported that sprouts grown in a pyramid lasted over a week without spoilage after harvesting, while controls only lasted twenty-four to thirty-six hours. In my backyard I planted several rows of carrots, radishes and lettuce and placed a four-foot-high pyramid over part of the garden. Photographs clearly show that the plants under the pyramid grew much larger than the others in the same time period.

Pyramid energy also affects taste beneficially. In the last chapter I mentioned the effect of a Manabox on water. The same effects occur when the water is placed in a pyramid, though generally not as quickly. I have achieved the best results when the water reaches the phi level. As with the Manabox and the orac, the taste of other liquids is altered when they are left within the pyramid. Solid foods are also affected. For the most part sweetness is enhanced, bitterness and sourness are greatly reduced, and flavor is improved. Many experiments indicate, however, that detection of taste differences varies greatly among individuals, which is well known. *Vril* does wonders for the sensitive palate and leaves indifferent palates indifferent.

Reports of the effect of pyramid energy on insects are intriguing. A number of researchers report that insects cannot stand the high vibrations of the energy, that they will not go inside a large pyramid. A few claim that the energy even kills insects. I do not know on what kind of tests or observations these claims are based, but as far as I know, there are not published reports of controlled experiments. All we have are anecdotes. One from my laboratory is that when I first began experimenting I had a terrible problem with roaches, which were barely kept at bay with insecticides. But after *vril* generators of various sorts began accumulating, the roaches suddenly disappeared. I do not know whether they could not tolerate the energy, whether the energy affected the fertilization of their eggs, or whether they just found a more comfortable home. The experience is interesting, but not conclusive by any means.

A little more scientific is an experiment carried out by one of my research correspondents. Two small bowls of grapes were cut in half and the seeds removed. One bowl was placed under a six-inch high pyramid, and the other was placed some distance away as a control. The experiment was designed to test the energy effect on the grapes, but a side effect eclipsed the importance of the original intention. Within twenty-four hours the bowl inside the pyramid hosted a happy colony of fruit flies, while the bowl outside had none. Even stranger, when a Manabox was placed about eighteen inches from the pyramid, the flies left to settle on the box, apparently attracted by the stronger energy output.

## Nonorganic Effects

In a mood of "try anything once," I placed a tarnished silver half-dollar at the phi point in a clear pyramid. Nothing particularly unusual happened until I handled the coin. Then I noticed that the tarnish was easily wiped off with my finger. I did more experiments ranging in time from a few hours to several weeks, but never achieved better results than I did in a twenty-four hour period. At no time was the tarnish completely wiped off leaving a clean, shiny surface but was only loosened on the high relief of the coin. Later experiments produced the same phenomenon with other metals and other types of *vril* generators. It took only a few minutes for the effect to take place on copper sheeting, and within three hours very rusty steel nuts could be wiped down to the bare metal in spots. The energy seems to loosen tarnish and rust, but not evenly. Preliminary experiments with silver objects indicate that the energy also tends to slow down the tarnishing process.

Razor blade sharpening is the most famous effect of the pyramid shape. Here the energy seems to greatly speed up a natural process. The metal on the edge of a blade has a crystalline structure. It is a "live" structure in the sense that if you merely leave any blade alone for a long time it will gradually regain some of its original sharpness. Under the pyramid this process takes place within hours and keeps on for many days after many uses. Drbal, the discoverer of this effect, is said to have obtained two hundred shaves with a blue blade. I have obtained up to two hundred shaves with a platinum blade and one hundred with a blue blade kept in a pyramid, and up to seven hundred shaves with a blue blade on a high-powered Manaplate. With my latest *vril* devices I regularly use a throwaway blade for three to six months.

Sharpening effects have been noted under pyramids as small as three inches high, and positive results have been obtained with cutlery, scissors and even electric razors. It is known that the crystalline edge of a sharpened blade can absorb up to 22 percent of the blade's weight in water, and this causes it to become dull faster. Apparently the pyramid energy dehydrates the blade, and this is what restores the sharpness. Environmental humidity, orientation of the pyramid and orientation of the blade within the pyramid all affect the results.

## Physiological Effects

It was not long after the news of energy effects in the pyramid were made public that somebody decided to find out what it would do to a human being. This was not a new venture, of course. Napoleon slept overnight in the Great Pyramid once and refused to talk about it, and the writer Paul Brunton reported astral travel experiences during his stay. Starting in the 1970s, however, people no longer had to go to Egypt to explore the deeper mysteries of the pyramid. They could build or buy their own, and so they did, for meditating, sleeping and even wearing.

The physiological effects of spending time in the pyramid energy field differ with individuals. The most common effect reported is one of feeling "charged up" and full of energy. The longer one stays inside, the more one feels "saturated" and eventually uncomfortable. Some people then get very drowsy and must sleep, after which they feel very refreshed. The effects sound very similar to those Reich claimed for his orac. A sensitive person sitting below the apex of a meditation pyramid usually feels an energy sensation zipping up or down the spine, and the meditation experience is greatly enhanced. To some it feels like the "third eye" is opening, and there are many reports of clairvoyant, telepathic and out-of-body experiences and lucid dreaming. Other than psychic effects, many people report the easing of pain from headaches and arthritis, the lowering of blood pressure, increased sexual drive and, in general, the same healing effects reported by Reich with his oracs. On the other hand, some people report increased headaches and pain, nausea and general discomfort, even from a short stay in a pyramid. And, of course, there are those who report no particular sensations at all.

The first researchers in this area used fairly large pyramids, at least six feet high, thinking logically that you had to be inside the pyramid to get the effects. Later it was discovered that a pyramid about the size of a hat could be worn and produce all the effects of a large one. In an article I described my experience with a pyramid cap:

> *Curious to see what effect the energy might have on the mind, I meditated with an open-base, six-inch pyramid on my head. I did this late at night, of course, in order to avoid some friendly family jeering. The effects were remarkable. At first, the pyramid seemed to be rolling around on my head and I had to touch it to make sure it wasn't really moving. A few moments later, it seemed to grow tighter until it felt like a close-fitting cap. After that my mind's eye was swamped with a swift series of dream-like sequences of great clarity, but no comprehensible meaning. Unrecognizable characters walked about and seemed to be talking in a normal setting. In seconds the scene changed. It was much like being shown a succession of motion picture film clips stuck together without rhyme or reason.*

Even later, it was found that a small pyramid suspended above an area produced most of the effects below it. So for about eleven years my wife and I slept with a four-foot high metal pyramid suspended above the bed, and I worked with a ten-inch high pyramid suspended over my desk. We enjoyed abundant personal energy and excellent health, which we attributed to the pyramid. Now we use other energy devices instead of pyramids.

Because of the pyramid's unique properties, a number of people have built pyramid-shaped structures to live, play and work in. Some state and county governments have built picnic shelters in the pyramid form, and there are several pyramid-shaped churches around the country. When I have set up pyramid frames in a park, children and animals tend to use them as a temporary resting place. I know of a dentist who had a pyramid built over her dental chair and claimed that it lessened her patients' pain. I know of a hair salon in Southern California (where else) that had pyramids over each chair and even produced its own shampoo in a pyramid-shaped bottle, because they claimed that the pyramid energy helped to promote the health and beauty of a person's hair. Since the pyramid fad of the 1970s quite a few architects have incorporated pyramid shapes into offices, shopping centers and conference halls, generally as skylights, but their intentions are not known.

I know of no studies on the effects of consistently living in a pyramid structure, but Patrick Flanagan reported an incident in which a cat was placed in a pyramid once a day for a half-hour. The cat got to like the pyramid so much he began to sleep in it. After six weeks, according to the story, the cat became a vegetarian and refused to eat meat. I have to say that eleven years of sleeping under a pyramid did not produce that effect on me.

### Electronic Effects

No one has yet figured out a way to effectively measure *vril* with electronic instruments, even though the energy does affect electronic devices. A California researcher writing in *The Pyramid Guide,* a newsletter of the 1970s and 1980s, described an experiment with a television set. His black-and-white set was getting poor reception, so he suspended a nine-inch base aluminum pyramid directly over the picture tube. Nothing happened immediately, but within two weeks the picture had improved noticeably, and by the end of three weeks the reception was very good. Thinking that weather might have caused the change or alterations in the components, he experimented with a color set. Two channels which had given poor reception cleared up, while the two best channels began to come only in black and white. Other channels were not affected at all. When the pyramid was taken down the set returned to its previous condition. Then he used two pyramids, hooking one to each of the antenna lead-ins, with the roof antenna completely disconnected. All channels came in strong, but the picture was blurred and the colors had a tendency to shift and fluctuate.

Another researcher claimed that his pyramid powered a "tube-type vibratonic communication device." He said there was a pickup at the focal point and no switch. Still another report said that a battery-operated watch left near a pyramid lost half an hour daily unless it was stored well away from the model. In early 1973 reporters attempting to take pictures inside a twelve-foot high pyramid noted that their light meter registered light inside the dark pyramid and failed to register at all when taken back into the sun.

In the last chapter I mentioned the effect of a pyramid on battery-charging. In a different type of experiment, a researcher bought four new batteries and left two on the shelf while "charging" the other two in a pyramid for a week. Then he put both sets in flashlights and left them on for four hours until their light was very dim. Both flashlights were then left off for a week and tested again. The control batteries (those on the shelf) would not light and were found to have leaked. The "pyramid" batteries lit up with about 50 percent brightness. After leaving the "pyramid" flash-lights alone for a month, he tested them again, and there was no light. But when the batteries had been "charged" again in a pyramid for twenty-four hours, they produced about 25 percent of the original bright-ness. Another forty-eight-hour charge did not increase the brightness, but another week's charge caused the batteries to produce one final camera-like flash before they quit for good. All in all, it was estimated that the pyramid-charged batteries produced light three times as long as the controls.

While standing on top of the Great Pyramid with a companion and some Arab guides, Sir W. Siemens, a British inventor, noted that whenever his hand was raised with the fingers outspread he could hear an acute ringing noise. Curious, he converted a bottle into a Leyden jar (which accumulates static electricity) and held it over his head. Sparks began to fly from the neck of the bottle. The guides became fearful and threatened him, so Siemens lowered the bottle toward one of them. It gave the guide such a shock that he was knocked to the ground. In 1980 I spent the night of the vernal equinox combined with the full moon on top of the Great Pyramid. While I did not have a Leyden jar to produce dramatic effects, I did experience a power-ful sense of tingling and being charged with energy. I have felt the same sensations on top of Dome Rock in Yosemite. That large and isolated granite outcropping picks up a strong static charge in dry weather just before a storm. The Great Pyramid is also a large, iso-lated limestone "outcropping" in a very dry area. Is this static effect usual for limestone? Some kind of electronic effects are obviously taking place, but only more research will determine what they are for sure.

### Psychic Effects

Effects detected by psychical perception are not easily demonstrable, but so many similar things have been reported from different sources that the most consistent ones should be considered.

One of the earliest researchers in this area was Verne Cameron, a well-known dowser. Using a dowsing device he called an "aurameter" (fully described in Chapters 6 and 7), he detected an upward flow of energy from the tip of a pyramid, apparently accompanied by a simultaneous downward flow. Many others, including many of my experimental subjects, have detected the same thing. To most it feels as if a cool breeze is flowing against the fingers and palm as they are held over the tip of the pyramid. Usually tingling is also felt. These are virtually the same sensations reported by Reichenbach and Reich with their materials.

This beam of energy supposedly travels upward for an unknown distance. This has led some to speculate that a similar beam projects from the Great Pyramid and could possibly serve as a homing signal to spacecraft. This may be far-fetched, but something is surely projecting or radiating from the top of pyramids, including the Great Pyramid. In a number of experiments, subjects have detected sensations from pyramids placed under their chairs without their knowledge, apparently from the energy beaming from the tip.

The tip is not the only portion of a pyramid that emits a beam of energy. *Vril* beams have been felt by psychics or sensitives from every point. The consensus is that the corners of a pyramid seem to emit more energy than the flat panels, but the pyramid itself seems surrounded by a field of energy in dynamic motion that has a pronounced bulge toward the north. This energy projection from corners as well as the field effect are common enough in static electric generators. Pyramid energy shares many but not all the characteristics of static electricity. Static electricity itself contains mysteries and its relationship to pyramid energy may be closer than we think.

Cameron discovered another curious fact about pyramids that has been borne out by many experiments. With his dowsing instrument he detected an invisible pyramid extending downward from all sides of a pyramid model, as if the model were the capstone of a much larger pyramid. It is not known how far down the invisible pyramid extends, but it is at least to the ground. After detecting the unseen shape myself, I wondered if there might also be an energy reaction inside this invisible pyramid. I held a six-inch base model pyramid about two feet over the heads of a number of subjects. They reported sensations identical to those of being inside a full-scale meditation pyramid. This was not due to suggestion as the subject did not know exactly when the pyramid model was over his or her head.

Clairvoyants claim to be able to see an aura around the pyramid as well as emanations from the corners and apex. Their descriptions remind one greatly of what was seen by Reichenbach's sensitives and by Reich in his dark basement: swirling blue vapor, flashes of light, and occasionally a rainbow of colors.

## The Companions of Cheops

The energy effects in the inner chambers of the Great Pyramid of Cheops have been extensively described. Directly below the apex are: the King's Chamber with its granite walls and capacitor-like roof structure; the

Queen's Chamber below it with its limestone walls thickly encrusted with salt; and the Pit, carved deep into the bedrock where tiny quartz crystals are growing. However, there are many other pyramids on the Giza Plateau above the town that are equally as important and probably as powerful. Because the "companions of Cheops" are so little known, I would like to describe experiences with these two pyramids.

Directly to the southwest of Cheops is the Second Pyramid, attributed to Kephren, or Khafre, for no reason except that he was pharoah after Cheops. From the ground it looks like a twin to Cheops in size and shape, but it is about two-and-a-half feet shorter in its present state. Like Cheops, it lacks a capstone, and it is estimated that it would be ten feet shorter than Cheops if both were complete. Unlike Cheops, it is built at a slightly steeper angle of 52 or 53 degrees, and the apex angle is about 72 degrees. Also unlike Cheops, it still has a fair amount of the original outer casing stones near the top, made of polished limestone. Around the base is a course of original casing blocks in red granite, another difference from Cheops whose lower courses, at least, were of polished limestone. No one knows how far up the granite courses reached on Kephren or why two types of stone were used. In the Great Pyramid eight "cartouches" or name glyphs of Cheops were found in the spaces above the King's Chamber, but Kephren's name was found only once in the temple outside the Second Pyramid. Nevertheless, I will call it Kephren for convenience.

There are two entrances to this pyramid, both on the north. One is fifty feet above the base and the other is hewn out of the bedrock a few yards in front of the pyramid itself. These days you enter through this second entrance. After the gatekeeper tears your ticket, you descend at a half crouch through a narrow cor-

ridor at a 22 degree angle for sixty or seventy feet. At
that point you can stand in a horizontal section about
thirty feet long. Midway to the east a short downward
slope leads to a chamber thirty-four feet long by ten
feet wide and eight feet high. Those who are sensitive
can tell that the energy is quite strong in this room.
Unfortunately, so is the stench. The sound resonance
of this room is exceptional, particularly the low tones
which reverberate for a very long time.

The horizontal passage leads further to a steep slope
which rises to meet another horizontal passage coming
from the upper entrance. This continues south until
reaching a large chamber about forty-six feet long
(east/west) by sixteen feet wide by twenty-two feet high.
This is larger than any of the chambers in Cheops. It is
carved smoothly out of the bedrock, except for the
gabled roof made of limestone slabs angled to match
the face of the pyramid. This room is directly under
the apex of the pyramid, and the energy intensity is
quite high, but the air is fresh and invigorating as if
it were charged with negative ions. At the west end of
the room sits a fine granite coffer, apparently the same
size as the one in Cheops, only in better shape. Originally this coffer, which runs north/south, was set into
the floor, its top level with the granite floor stones, but
for some reason most of the blocks in the west half of
the room have been removed. This makes it two feet
lower than the other half and leaves just six blocks to
surround the coffer. A broken lid of thick granite leans
against the coffer on the west side. The room resonates
most strongly to a high note.

Here is where my friends and I made a remarkable
discovery. One of our group happened to place a hand
inside the coffer and immediately noticed a rather
bright violet glow around it which shimmered as the
hand was shaken. Everyone in our group tried it, and

all could see the glow clearly. Shortly, two unknown tourists wandered into the chamber and both of them saw the light clearly. Later experiments showed that the light intensified with sound resonance. I am convinced that this light can be photographed, but we did not have the proper equipment at the time. Later my friends and I tried the same experiment in the coffer of Cheops, and it worked, though the light was not as bright there. This room in Kephren was the site of the highly controversial cosmic ray scan in 1968, conducted by Dr. Luis Alvarez and supported by twelve United States and international agencies. According to reports at the time, the results of the scan defied the laws of physics.

Almost a thousand yards southwest of Kephren lies the smaller pyramid of Mykerinos or Menkurah, named after another pharaoh. It is less than half as high as the other two and is also missing a capstone. One wonders whether—in spite of psychic visions describing capstones of gold, marble or crystal—these pyramids were ever intended to have capstones. Sixteen or so of the lower courses of Mykerinos are faced with red granite blocks in a rough, pillowed finish. It would appear from the large number of blocks piled around the area that the entire structure may have been covered with them.

The entrance is a short way above the base on the north side and descends steeply into the bedrock. There a horizontal passage opens into a sort of antechamber with a curious design on the east and west walls that reminded me of a maze or labyrinth. This feature is startling because in neither of the other two pyramids is there any trace of designs or drawings ever having been on their walls. This design intrigued me because I also found it in the mortuary temple of Cheops, on the tablet in front of the Sphinx, on many

Old Kingdom sarcophagi, at Karnak and at the necropolis of Hatepshut (thought to be the Queen of Sheba). Egyptologists call it simply a "panel decoration," but it obviously has a much deeper significance. If it is a maze, it ties in directly to ancient wisdom about earth energies.

The passage narrows again after the antechamber and runs into a fairly large and long room on an east/west line. Toward the west end of this room a short flight of steps leads down to an oddly-angled room with six "storerooms" cut into it. This rather smallish room is approximately diagonal to the other rooms and passages of the pyramid, which, like those of Cheops and Kephren, are aligned to the points of the compass. The "storerooms" (in which nothing was ever found) reminded me of the holes of a harmonica. The room does resonate very strongly to a low note.

At the very west end of the upper room is another chamber with its length north/south. It is lined entirely with polished red granite blocks set into the carved bedrock, and the roof is high and rounded. The room resonates beautifully and strongly to a high note. There was once a basalt coffer in it "carved with panel decorations," (Edwards) but it was lost at sea on its way to England.

Based on my visits and research, I made three hypotheses: a) Mykerinos was the first of the Giza group of pyramids to be built, Kephren was next as an improvement, and Cheops was the final improvement that "worked" (for whatever purpose); b) the final plan made use of all three as an interacting complex; and c) apart from any astronomical, mathematical or geodetic use, these pyramids were primarily intended as *vril* generators designed to use sound as an amplifying principle.

Ancient pyramids of various kinds can be found in the United States, Mexico, Central and South America and, supposedly, Asia. I have experienced *vril* effects at many of them, but whether that was part of their intended purpose or not just is not known.

## Experimenting on Your Own

There are many formulas for constructing pyramid models based on the measurements of the Great Pyramid in Egypt. Some are more complicated than others, and they vary considerably in terms of duplicating the exact proportions of the original. However, I have found that for producing the effects discussed above, considerable variation is tolerable. Of the many methods available, these are the easiest to follow:

1. *The basic six-inch-high model.* This is the most convenient for research. Cut four triangles out of any material you choose, with a base of 9⅜″ and sides of 8⅞″. Place the triangles flat on a table with the sides adjacent, tape them together, fold them into the pyramid shape, and tape the open side shut.

2. *The percentage method.* In this case, if you consider the length of the base of one triangle to be X, then the sides are X - 5%. A triangle with a base of 10″ would have sides of 9.5″ and the height would be 6.4″. Using the metric system might make the calculations easier.

3. *The 3-4-5 method.* Built to scale in inches, this pyramid would be 4″ high, with a 6″ base. To construct, draw a line 6″ long, bisect it with a line 5″ high, and connect the far end of the 5″ line to each end of the 6″ line. Cut four such triangles and assemble as above. By multiplying the proportions you can get pyramids of various sizes.

4. *The 7-11 method.* This is similar to the previous method but is preferred by some because of the mystical significance of the numbers. It calls for 7″ of pyramid height for every 11″ of base length. To calculate it draw a right triangle with a base of 5.5″ and a height of 7″. The remaining side (the hypotenuse) will be 8⅛″. Next draw four triangles with an 11″ base bisected by a line 8⅞″ high, with lines drawn from the top of that line to the ends of the 11″ line; cut and assemble. Multiply the proportions to get various sizes.

5. *The phi method.* This was my discovery, for fanatics of exactitude. Pick any base size you want and divide it in half. Multiply that number by 1.618 and you get the proper height for each triangular panel. Then draw lines from the end of that line to the ends of the base line, cut and assemble as above. Since the measurement will come out to several decimal places, this method works well with the metric system. Rounding off your answer to the nearest inches or feet will give you a very close approximation. After all, even the Great Pyramid is not exact.

6. *The equilateral method.* This is the easiest of all. Just draw and cut out four triangles with equal bases and sides, cut and assemble. It will look a little different, but the effects will be the same.

7. *Framework method #1.* Find dimensions for the size triangle you want and prepare four base lengths and four edge lengths out of metal, wood or plastic rods or tubing. Then obtain flexible plastic tubing that will fit snugly around your rigid rods or tubing. Cut six pieces about 2-3″ long and four pieces 1-2″ long. With nuts and bolts or pop rivets join one end of the short pieces to the center of four longer pieces to form four base joints. Then join the two remaining long pieces center to center, like a cross, to form the apex joint. Connect the base sections of the pyramid to the four

long/short flexible joints with the short ends sticking up; insert the four edge lengths into those joints at the base, and then use the apex joint to connect the four edge lengths at the top.

8. *Framework method #2.* A popular commercial method, this requires the use of stiff metal wire or rod. First cut one piece four times the length of your chosen base, bend it into a square and glue or weld it together. It's easier if you bend the metal so that the ends come together at the middle of one side. Then cut two pieces which are double the length of the triangle edge determined by one of the methods above. If you choose the percentage method for a pyramid with a 10" base, for instance, you would cut one base piece 40" long (4x10) and two edge pieces 19" long (2x9.5). With your base square already made, bend each edge piece in two so that the ends reach two adjacent corners of the base. Glue or weld them there. Finally, glue or weld together the bends of the edge pieces where they meet at the top.

### Amplifying the Power

Experimenters are always seeking for ways to amplify the power of a pyramid. Magnets, crystals or managizers (my generic term for Manaboxes, Manaplates and similar devices) placed inside will amplify well, particularly at the corners or in the center. Placing a pyramid on a Manaplate the size of its own base is very good, too, as is constructing the pyramid in layers like an orac.

A very interesting modification actually duplicates the Great Pyramid more closely than most models. The Great Pyramid is more of a trapezoid than a pointed pyramid. If it originally had a capstone, it would have been about 1 percent taller. If you cut off up to 5 percent of the top of your pyramid, you will have a platform on top for experiments and some different effects as well. When I did this on a pyramid meditation cap, I experienced a sudden sense of down-rushing energy quite different from that of a pointed pyramid.

The pyramid is a fascinating and versatile *vril* device with many more variations than I have been able to describe here. Unfortunately, when it became a commercial product in the 1970s so many manufacturers jumped onto the bandwagon and so many wild claims were made for its powers that the market was saturated and the public finally became too skeptical. So all across the country there are numerous varieties of pyramids languishing in closets, attics, basements and even warehouses. Perhaps someone's children or grandchildren might take them out and use them again in ways that will be beneficial.

# 6
# Radionics: Detecting Subtle Radiation?

The term "radionics" means different things to different people. It can include such things as dowsing for water, oil or gold; diagnosing diseases from a drop of blood or sample of hair; and detecting subtle radiations emitted by objects.

In this chapter I define radionics as the art and science of determining the nature and quality of things, using tools and instruments to receive real or apparent radiations from those things. Such a definition includes several overlapping fields, such as dowsing, radiesthesia and machine radionics. Here I discuss only "passive radionics," the receiving of information. "Active radionics," covering things like radionics "treatment," is covered in the next chapter. In this chapter I concentrate on the tools used in the hope that this will shed more light on the subject. Some of my information is at odds with what others have written, and some of it may be quite new.

## Dowsing with the Pendulum

A pendulum, as most of you know, is a weight hung from a string, cord or wire. It is used in many ways:

by carpenters and surveyors as a plumb bob; by some psychotherapists to retrieve subconscious information; by some hypnotists to help put people into trance; and by some mediums to contact spirits. However, here we investigate reports that the pendulum reacts to radiations coming from people, objects and even symbols.

Consider the use of the pendulum for dowsing water. The tool itself is merely a weight hanging from a line. It can range from a simple ring dangling from a thread to a complex, secretly-fashioned alloyed ovoid with a special compartment, attached to a chain. The line is held by the operator, usually between the thumb and forefinger, with the weight naturally hanging earthward. The length of the line generally varies from four to ten inches. Many operators claim that the pendulum is sensitive to radiations and that it responds to them by gyrating and moving in certain ways. The operator interprets these movements to gain information about the nature and quality of the radiation or of its source.

In locating water the operator walks across a likely area holding the pendulum in front of him or her. Its movement in a certain way shows that it is above a watercourse. Other movements indicate the depth and extent of the water supply, as well as its direction of flow and purity. Running water is supposedly easier to locate than still water, whether it is running freely through the ground or in a pipe. Explanations given by dowsers vary, but the general consensus is that water generates a peculiar radiation to which the pendulum/ operator combination is sensitive, and that running water generates this radiation in a greater degree. There are operators who are able to sense water without any kind of device at all, but there is no pendulum of any sort that will work without an operator. The sensitivity is in the operator, not in the pendulum. The latter is only a tool for objectifying what the operator is receiving. But that leaves the question of what it is that the operator is receiving.

The record of successes at water locating by using a pendulum or similar device, while certainly not 100 percent, is still far greater than by any other known method. A Catholic priest with whom I worked in West Africa located five thousand wells by dowsing in the country that used to be called Upper Volta. But is the radiation theory reasonable? If water were the only substance to which the operator/pendulum were sensitive, that theory might "hold water." However, it has been proven many times that *any* substance may be located with a pendulum. Water, oil, iron, gold, silver, uranium, crystals, bones, plastic, paper—all of these and more have been found by the same process. And consider that water has been located as deep as six hundred feet below ground by dowsing with a pendulum. That means that water radiation would have to penetrate through all the intervening layers of rock, minerals and other material and still be strong enough to affect the operator. What is more, the operator would have to be able to differentiate that particular radiation from all the others in between. It has been shown that one operator can go over a given territory and locate water, while another can go over the same territory looking for iron ore and completely miss the water. In other words, the operator finds only what he or she is looking for, if it is there.

Interviews with dowsers show that before starting to dowse they concentrate firmly and strongly on the subject of the search. In addition, the dowser has already established a "code" for the meaning of the pendulum movements. Whether consciously by decision or unconsciously by learning from another dowser, the operator has determined that certain motions of the pendulum mean certain things. The fact that different dowsers have different codes or interpretations for the same movements shows that the radiation and response are not strictly objective. Still, this does not rule out a special radiation in water, even though it does imply that certain people have an incredible ability to differentiate subtle variations in radiations from many substances merely by focusing the attention on one of them. It also implies that such radiations have tremendous energy in order to pass virtually unhindered through thousands of tons of other substances that have their own radiations.

What really knocks out the radiation theory is another pendulum use called "map dowsing." In this practice the operator holds the pendulum over a map of the area in question and is still able to locate the sought-for substance, even though it might be on the other side of the world. This method is well proven and has been used many times with great success. Vern Cameron, already mentioned, was prevented from traveling outside the United States during World War II because he had accurately located all of our submarines by map dowsing. I have used it myself to locate a wandering son, a stolen car and other things.

One might believe that a pendulum operator can sense radiation from a substance hundreds of feet below the ground underfoot. But it stretches credibility beyond the breaking point to suggest one can sense the radiation of a particular stream of water or underground oil hundreds or thousands of miles away. There has to be a better explanation.

### The *Huna* Theory

Not surprisingly, I have a theory to offer, based on the Hawaiian shaman tradition. I offer it only as a working hypothesis that covers more of the facts of pendulum experience.

First, I make three basic assumptions, two of which have already been discussed:

1. In agreement with Mesmer, I propose a universal essence or ether that permeates all things and can expand, contract and assume any pattern or shape. It can also be a medium for energy, as water is for waves, and for information, as air is for speech. To this essence I give the equivalent Hawaiian name of *aka*.

2. There is a universal energy which can be amplified or attenuated (weakened) within particular patterns of focus, direction, movement or form. While I could use the Hawaiian word *ola* for this, I use instead the generic term *vril*, which is already established.

3. There is a universal mind that expresses itself through individual minds, which have varying capacities to be aware of and influenced by both *aka* and *vril*. It will be easier to stick with the word "mind" for this one.

Note that we are not concerned at all with who or what might have created these things; we are just looking for a theory to explain certain experiences. These ideas appear in many traditions including the Hawaiian, but if you like, you can take them as a working model and see how well they explain the facts.

Using these assumptions, we can say that the pendulum operators use their minds to increase their *vril* and extend their *aka* (thinking of it as an aura might help) to connect with the *aka* pattern of what they are searching for. The search is conducted by an intense focus on the object of the search or on a question related to the object. Then a part of the operator's mind (call it subconscious) gives information about the pattern he or she has connected with. It does this by influencing his hand to move the pendulum according to a pattern or code which has meaning to the conscious part of his mind. The pendulum is moved, not by the effect upon it of certain radiations, but by micromuscular movements of the operator's own hand stimulated by a part of his own mind. I call this the *huna* theory, *huna* being the name for Hawaiian shamanic knowledge.

A good dowser, then, must have high energy (Cameron spoke of using an "auric charge"), high concentration (to ignore distractions), and high sensitivity (to be able to respond to subtle information sources). In regard to the latter, it is well known that emotional or physical stress, which always involves body tension, can greatly diminish a dowser's effectiveness. A clear mind and a relaxed body aid sensitivity.

## Medical Radiesthesia

The pendulum is used in another practice frequently referred to as medical radiesthesia. It is much more common in Europe than in the United States, where it is mostly frowned upon. In Europe it is used by medical doctors as well as folk healers.

Basically medical radiesthesia consists of diagnosing illness by holding the pendulum over areas of the body, asking the appropriate questions and interpreting the movements by a code similar to what dowsers use. Elaborate charts have been made to indicate the movements to be expected for various conditions in particular areas of the body. The usual theory is that diseased organs are radiating "distress signals" that influence the pendulum movement. By checking a chart or table, the diagnostician can determine which disease is involved.

According to the theory presented above, the chart obviously serves as a standard code which must be stored in subconscious memory before it can be used effectively. This idea is strengthened by the fact that there are charts which contradict each other, all of which work anyway. In addition, many practitioners of medical radiesthesia get equally good results by working with a photograph, a blood sample or a personal item of the patient's, which sounds similar to map dowsing. In France I witnessed a practitioner who used a photograph to correctly diagnose a back problem without having any previous knowledge of the patient. And while still in France I used a pendulum to correctly determine the time of birth and sex of a baby born in England. This was not a forecast, but a determination made several days after the event. All this strains the radiation theory severely, but it fits nicely with the *huna* theory.

## Detecting Fields

Another use for the pendulum is to measure the size, shape and intensity of energy fields around pyramids, oracs, Manaboxes, people and objects of any kind. A good pendulum for this purpose can be made from either a thin plastic ball of the type that contains toys in vending machines or a ping-pong ball, attached to a light thread about ten to fifteen inches long.

The effect is very strange. I tried this first with a pyramid, suspending the pendulum about two feet from the side and slowly drawing it in toward the pyramid to try to outline the energy field. At a distance of about one foot I began to feel a kind of resistance, as if the pendulum were actually pushing against something. It was like the sensation of pushing two similar poles of a magnet toward each other, only not as strong. The effect was more or less the same with all the other *vril* sources discussed above. By paying attention to the resistance sensation, I could outline the shape of the field around the source. Many different experiments with pendulums, sensitive subjects and organic sub-

stances revealed that the field extended far beyond
the point of resistance. That point just indicated the
intensity to which the pendulum (and my subconscious)
responded.

It is clear that both pendulum and operator are at
work here. Ordinarily, a pendulum at rest or in slow
movement hangs straight down. But when I brought
the pendulum through the field of a strong *vril* source,
it visibly moved out of the vertical, as if there were a
real physical resistance. It felt like moving the
pendulum through thicker air. This effect was most
noticeable when moving the pendulum between two
strong *vril* sources, such as two crystals or two
Managizer plates. Other factors that affected the
pendulum were my degree of conscious attention and
the weight of the pendulum. If I breathed deeply
beforehand, it seemed to increase the effect as well as
my own sensitivity. So this phenomenon is neither
physical nor psychic alone, but rather psychophysical.
Quite a number of experimenters have tried it with
similar results. In this case the effects of radiant energy
are affecting not only the operator but also the
pendulum.

## Measuring Psychic Vibrations

In his book *Psychometric Analysis,* Max Freedom
Long, an early author on *Huna,* discussed an instrument invented by Andre Bovis, the same man who first
discovered the pyramid energy effect. Bovis was a
professional dowser who used a pendulum to
determine whether casks of wine and wheels of cheese
were good or bad. Not satisfied with a simple
indication of their condition, he sought to improve his
method by devising an instrument that would give the
exact degree of quality. The result was the Bovis

Biometer, designed to measure the radiating waves of any object by means of a measuring stick and a pendulum. The stick was divided into "biometric degrees" of two centimeters each. Bovis found a number which, when multiplied by the number of degrees registered, would yield an answer in angstroms (units of wavelength of light), thus lending his theory some scientific credibility.

The device consisted of a flat piece of wood with a strip of mica at one end and a strip of iron at the other. A measuring ruler was fitted to slide under the end with the iron. A small cup attached to it would hold a sample of the material to be tested. On the ruler were marked 100 biometric degrees. For testing, the ruler was extended to the 100 degree mark with the sample in the cup. The pendulum was held over the iron and mica plates in turn. A clockwise swing over both indicated that the sample was in a perfect state. If a counterclockwise swing occurred over one end, the ruler with its attached sample was slowly brought in until two clockwise swings were recorded. At that point the degree mark, where the ruler went under the board, indicated the degree of perfection. A 70 degree reading indicated that the item was only 70 percent perfect. In later experiments a cord with a needle was attached to the end of the ruler, and this was then attached to a distant sample. This shot Bovis's wave theory, but it worked. In time the Biometer was used to diagnose physical ailments as well as the quality of cheese and wine. After World War I a physicist/ engineer by the name of Dr. Oscar Brunler obtained a Biometer and made several changes. He claimed that his version could measure brain waves and "the place in evolution of the soul."

As Max Long clearly saw, there were no wave radiations of any kind being measured by the Biometer. It was merely a handy device for permitting the sub-conscious to objectify information. One of the qualities found in *vril* is that it can be conducted through any medium including string and wood. According to *huna* theory, when a sample was attached to the Biometer, the operator's subconscious merely used this handy path through the *aka* to focus on the sample, obtain the required information and relay it through the pendulum according to the established code.

## Other Dowsing Devices

There are many devices used for dowsing besides the pendulum. The best known is probably the forked stick used by "water witches." When the dowser walks over an underground stream, the stick, which is held by the forked ends, is attracted downward. A number of cases have been reported in which the downward pull was so strong that the operator's hands were chafed when he or she tried to resist it. Although this sounds like a purely objective effect, it cannot be so, because another person walking over the same area with the same stick might get no effect at all.

From the *huna* theory, it would seem that the operator had accumulated a large amount of *vril* for subconscious use. The prearranged code was for the stick to dip over water. Given enough *vril*, the sub-conscious would be able to make the stick dip in spite of conscious resistance. This is not as strange as it sounds because dowsing sticks are typically held in a way that keeps them under tension. Another common dowsing device is a set of wire rods of varying length, bent at an angle to form handles. One of these is held in each hand with the long sections pointing forward as the operator walks along. Depending on the code, the rods either cross or separate over the object being sought. Some United States Marines in Vietnam were trained to use these with considerable success for locating enemy tunnels.

One of the most sensitive devices of this type is the Aurameter, invented by Verne Cameron. It is basically composed of a hollow aluminum handle to which is attached a length of piano wire, coiled in the center for greater flexibility, and ending in a weighted copper tip. It is an excellent tool for locating and outlining *vril* fields. I have used it extensively in experiments and have found nothing to surpass it.

One of the most interesting experiments in which the Aurameter was used involves *vril* fields apparently emanating from purely symbolic designs. Francis Drake, an experimenter, put a Maltese cross on one face of a pyramid merely to designate the north side. However, every time he placed his hand over the symbol, his hand began to tremble, as if some powerful force were coming from that side of the pyramid. Later tests by William Cox, a protégé of Cameron's, indicated that many symbolic forms seem to radiate their own peculiar energy patterns. I have verified this hundreds of times. The more traditional symbols, those that have been in use over the centuries, apparently have the strongest emissions. No one can say whether this is because of their use, their triggering of subconscious associations, or their relation to basic patterns of the universe. The pendulum can be used to detect these fields, but the Aurameter gives a much better indication of their shape and intensity.

The question is, where is the energy coming from? The pyramid is a three-dimensional form that accumulates or generates energy simply because of its shape. Can it be that a two-dimensional form does the same thing? The latest research suggests that this is so. Some two-dimensional patterns are even stronger than most pyramids or crystals and produce all the same effects. Here is an area that is wide open for more research.

## Radionics Machines

Imagine an electronic device that allows you to analyze the physical properties of any object, even down to the atomic level; to diagnose any illness without lab tests or surgery; or to evaluate a person's personality or potential without any tests. Imagine further that the physical object or person need not even be present, that a photograph or a sample of blood, saliva or hair will do just as well. Imagine even further that the device does not have to be hooked up to electricity to work. Then really stretch your mind to imagine that even the physical device is not necessary.

Sound wild? I have described what are generally known as radionics machines. Basically these consist of an electronic-like machine, a set of coded "rate sheets" or lists of qualities or characteristics, and a skilled operator. These were popular even with physicians in the 1940s and 1950s. I used an old "Hunter" brand machine from the forties, as big as an organ and packed with dials and spinning lights. However, various legal problems have driven most of these machines into basements and attics or under lock and key. They are still around, but no one is using them legally for medical diagnosis. Two of the best known types of radionics machines are described below, as well as some simpler variations.

## The Hieronymous Machine

On September 27, 1949, Patent Number 2,482,773 was issued for an unusual device whose expressed purpose was to detect, identify and analyze radiations which

emanate from every known chemical element. This
device was presented as a chemical and mineral analyzer. The patent application stated that the radiations
were "probably" electrons. It was claimed that they
occur at ordinary room temperatures and that they had
electrical and optical characteristics and frequencies
disposed in the violet to ultraviolet portion of the
spectrum. Further, it was stated that these radiations
"or their effects" could be carried over electrical conductors and that they could be affected by electrical
capacity inductance and resistance. They could also be
refracted, focused, diffracted and otherwise manipu-
lated in the same way as light.

This invention was the now famous Hieronymous
Machine, invented by Thomas G. Hieronymous. The
first point to notice is the great similarity between the
effects of what Hieronymous came to call "eloptic"
radiations (electrical/optical) and the effects of animal
magnetism and od, as reported by Mesmer and
Reichenbach.

The Hieronymous Machine was composed of five
units. First was a unit designed to hold the sample and
receive the radiations. The receptor was either a coil or
an electrode placed in close proximity to the sample.
The next unit was an analyzer or tuner, consisting of
two variable condensers, two electrodes, a prism and a
scale to indicate atomic weights. The eloptic rays were
supposed to run from the first unit through a wire to
the second unit, ending at the first electrode. This was
placed at the beginning of an opaque, insulated
passageway. The rays were supposed to travel along
this passage into a prism at the other end and be
refracted outward. The second electrode was intended
to pick up the ray at an angle indicated on the scale,
the theory being that the rays of each element would
refract at a different angle. The third unit was a

variable resistance, connected to the fourth by a transformer. The transformer was a conventional radio frequency amplifier said to amplify the eloptic rays and feed them into the fifth unit, the detector. Now this is where it gets interesting. The detector consisted of a plastic-coated metal plate or coil, over which the operator of the machine rubbed a finger or palm. The element being tested was identified when the operator's fingers encountered stiff resistance while rubbing, as if the plastic had turned to sticky glue. At that point the calibrated electrode in the second unit indicated the atomic number of the element just detected. A substance containing more than one element supposedly could be detected because of the peculiar composite frequency of the combination.

In practice, the detector plate was rubbed and the scale pointer turned by the operator until his or her fingers met the greatest resistance. Then the two variable condensers were turned and the plate rubbed again to the greatest point of resistance. Then the scale pointer was adjusted again for very fine tuning. Hieronymous admitted in his application that he did not know what caused the drag on the fingers.

The whole procedure sounds scientific and objective, but what Hieronymous really patented was an ingenious device to assist psychic perception. I could spend several pages pointing out anomalies in the circuitry, but instead I will emphasize just two points. First, although the machine was designed to be plugged into a 110V outlet, it was found to work equally well if not plugged in at all. Second, another very ingenious man discovered that all an operator needed was a symbol of the machine for it to work.

In an article for the science section of *Astounding Science Fiction,* which I remember reading in the 1950s, editor John Campbell wrote about his experiences with the strange device. After building a

Hieronymous Machine and satisfying himself that it did work, and without current, Campbell streamlined the setup almost to the ultimate. He drew a circuit diagram in India ink on standard drafting paper. In place of a real prism, he cut out a triangle to represent the prism and mounted it on a vernier (scaled down) dial. The spiral coil of the detector plate was also drawn in ink on paper and pasted to the back of a panel. It was connected to a symbolized vacuum tube through a condensor symbol by means of nylon thread. "The machine works beautifully, the consistency of performance is excellent," he wrote. Campbell discovered that the original machine would not work if one of the parts was defective, and neither would his symbolic machine work if part of the drawing was erased or if a thread was disconnected.

Let's look a little closer at the operation of the device. One thing Hieronymous failed to mention in his patent —possibly on purpose—was that it was necessary for the operator to *concentrate* on the element he was looking for. This sounds like dowsing, but with the drag of the fingers on the detector plate replacing the movements of a pendulum or other device. My experiments with Hieronymous-type instruments suggest that the inventor and other radionics experimenters are making a vital mistake when they believed that radiations were traveling from the sample through the circuitry to the operator. According to *huna* theory, the operation works the other way around. When the operator concentrates, his or her subconscious sends out an "*aka* finger," to the sample. That is, the operator extends awareness through the *aka* field following the line of circuitry. The *aka* finger finds what the operator is looking for or not and reports back by means of a physical sensation, the drag on the fingers. It has been amply shown that the surface of the detector plate does not undergo any objective physical change. The drag must be produced by subconsciously induced additional finger pressure, as subtle as the subconsciously induced swings of a pendulum. The circuitry itself forms part of the code, and the subconscious respects it because the conscious mind has accepted it. If the circuitry, in metal or ink, is broken, the subconscious message does not cross that point as long as the operator remains bound by the belief that proper circuitry is important.

The various dials used for tuning do not filter anything. Instead they simply allow the subconscious to give the operator more information. It is possible, however, that the condensers serve another function as well. You may recall that a Manaplate or orgone device is constructed along the lines of a condenser or capacitor. A variable condenser, then, is an adjustable orgone device that generates more or less energy as the plates are brought into or out of proximity. The condensers in the Hieronymous circuit could put additional *vril* power into the operation. It has been shown that dowsing devices work more accurately if additional *vril* (or prana or oxygen) is available. This can be achieved if the operator uses special breathing exercises or if a *vril* generating unit is added to the device. A radionics expert in India, Dr. B. Ghattacharyya, inventor of a number of magnetic dowsing devices, recognized this need for *vril* indirectly when he stated that "the more powerful the magnetic field, the more accurate the reading." Magnets, as already seen, are good generators of *vril.* The detector plate of the original Hieronymous Machine, because of its construction, is what I would call a 1x Manaplate.

### The De la Warr Device

George De la Warr, a British researcher, developed a number of radionics instruments in his laboratories.

One such device fits neatly into a briefcase, in which a diagnostic chart lies on the left and the instrument itself on the right. At the top of the instrument are two wells, designated "male" and "female." There is a detector device at the lower right of the instrument. It is a hollow cavity covered with a rubber membrane over which the fingers can be rubbed. After the proper response is received through this device, a "witness" sample, often of blood, saliva or hair, is put into one of the wells. A witness is a sample that is believed to resonate with whatever it came from. The operator mentally asks a question as the detector is rubbed. A "no" response is indicated by a smooth rub across the membrane, while a "yes" response is indicated by the membrane "sticking" to the fingers or bunching up.

It has been theorized that radiations from the witness resonate in the hollow cavity and cause an upward pressure when a question meriting a positive response is asked. But it should be clear from the description of the action of the Hieronymous detector that this is only another technique for allowing the subconscious to respond physically to the demand for information.

Between the two witness wells is a magnet attached to a rotating dial. Further mental questions and responses determine the proper setting for the magnet to be tuned into "overall resonance with the basic wavefield of the patient." A set of dials, which may be either variable condensers or resistors, are set at a previously determined frequency, corresponding to the patient's condition. An "effectiveness" dial records how far advanced the condition is or how effective is the operation of the body part in question, much like Bovis' ruler did. To carry out the diagnosis, a series of questions is laid on the lefthand chart. A probe attached to the instrument is touched to each question as a yes or no response is recorded by the fingers on the membrane. By a process of elimination, the possibilities are narrowed down and remedies are recommended.

De la Warr eventually developed a modification of this device that included a camera attachment, and he proceeded to do some "impossible" things. By means of a blood sample he was able to concentrate on a subject and record *on film* either the whole person or a designated part of the body. In one case he concentrated on his wedding day of thirty years previous with a blood sample from him and his wife in the wells. A picture of a couple in old-fashioned wedding outfits appeared on the film. In similar experiments with a lily seed, the operator concentrated on the future. He developed one picture that showed a bulb and another that showed a lily in full bloom. How could a resonating radiation theory explain a photograph of the future? Or of the past? Advocates try to explain by discussing the concept of humans as the cosmos in miniature, cells and atoms being miniature reflections of the cosmos as well. Thus, they contain the essence of all that has been and the potential of all that will be.

I believe the explanation in this case is simpler. Perhaps the film was not affected by the radiations from the object or the witness, but by the *aka* field of the operator's subconscious energized by *vril.* Given enough *vril,* the subconscious can move physical matter without the operator directly touching it. Experiments in the United States and Russia have demonstrated this. In the case of the photograph of the past, maybe De la Warr's own subconscious, storehouse of his memory, merely recalled the past and somehow was able to manipulate the chemical elements of the film medium to form an image of the memory. In the case of the seed, the subconscious might have reached out to investigate the physical properties of the seed and then projected onto the film its *probable* development at the time period being considered. This explanation attributes a lot of power to the subconscious. Shamanistic practices prove that the subconscious *is* far more powerful than most people can imagine.

## Working with Witnesses

As mentioned, in the field of radionics, a "witness" refers to an object or part of an object that is supposed to radiate energy in resonance with the original, as the vibrations of high C and low C resonate on the piano. Some dowsing rods have compartments to hold tiny samples of water, oil, gold or whatever the dowser is looking for, and these are called witnesses (or links). The idea is based on an ancient metaphysical concept that "like attracts like." Mineral samples, blood, saliva and hair are therefore logical choices for witnesses. However, photographs and signatures work just as well. You might justify this by saying that photographs and signatures are at least records of the original vibration. But even *symbols* of the original work just as well for witnesses, as in map dowsing. This suggests the shamanic idea that, since everything is already connected anyway, a symbol of the original is all you need for focus and contact. In radionics you can use anything you want to represent what you are tuning in to: figurines, crystals, coins, words, drawings, etc. The key is focus, not a physical or metaphysical connection.

## Rate Sheets

Among some radionics practitioners rate sheets are treated as if they have magical powers. They may be kept highly secret and shared with only a select few, sold for very high prices, or stolen by thieves who think they now have something valuable. Actually, a rate sheet is nothing more than a list of qualities or characteristics numbered in a way that corresponds to the tuner being used. In a typical example, for a machine with two dials, a rate sheet for emotions might look something like this:

### 1. Anger
    1.1 - Rage
    1.2 - Resentment
    1.3 - Guilt
    1.4 - Jealousy
    1.5 - Hate

The first dial, in conjunction with the detector plate, is used to help the operator discover whether anger is a factor in a person being checked. The second dial is used to determine what kind of anger. A third dial could even be used to refine the answer further, e.g., 1.1.1 - Rage at oneself; 1.1.2 - Rage at a family member; and so on. Or, after the first dial keys into the general category of anger, it can be used again for the next level of checking. Some radionics people are secretive about their rate sheets because they think they have discovered an actual, objective, immutable frequency rate relating to the topic in question. They do not understand that all they have done is establish a useful code for their subconscious.

Since all rate sheets are arbitrary, you can easily make up your own. Just list the kinds of things you want to look for and assign a number to each item. Then relate these numbers to your tuner. You can use the same numbers over and over for different lists simply by telling yourself to switch to a new search topic when you want to. Here are some rate sheet ideas to get you started:

## Yin/Yang Energies

1. Yin-Yin (extreme yin)
2. Yin (excessive yin)
3. Yin/Yang (harmony)
4. Yang (excessive yang)
5. Yang-Yang (extreme yang)

## Simplified Positive Bach Remedy Evaluation

1. Peace of mind - White Chestnut
2. Independence - Walnut
3. Motivation - Wild Rose
4. Fortitude - Olive
5. Love - Holly
6. Confidence - Rescue Remedy
7. Optimism - Gorse

## Body Areas (add subcategories as desired)

1. Head
2. Left arm
3. Right arm
4. Torso
5. Hips
6. Left leg
7. Right leg

### Keep It Simple

Although John Campbell streamlined the Hieronymous Machine "almost to the ultimate," the ultimate streamlining was done by a doctor who wrote that he had done away with the machine entirely! He got the same effects by rubbing his fingers on a table and concentrating on what he wanted to know. But many people are fascinated with physical tools and work better with them, even though the real power is in the operator and not the tools. In the field of radionics the tools do serve the highly practical purpose of helping to fine-tune the focus of the operator's mind.

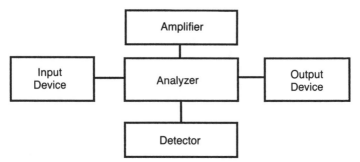

Basic set-up for a radionics machine

The basic components of a radionics machine are: a) an input device to receive "radiations" or information from the object of interest; b) an amplifier to increase the energy of the input signal; c) a tuner to narrow down the input to specifics; and d) a detector plate. There may also be an output device, discussed in Chapter 7.

For the technologically oriented, here are descriptions of two simple, inexpensive radionics "machines" that I have found to be just as effective as the more elaborate and expensive commercial models.

1. *The Radionics Radio.* Use a small, portable AM/FM radio with an antenna. The antenna is the input device, so place the witness or link touching or just pointing at the end of it. The volume control is the amplifier, and the station tuner the input tuner. For a detector plate, you can use a clear space on the body of the radio or plug in the earphone and attach it to an object suitable for rubbing. An empty audio cassette box stuffed with aluminum foil or steel wool, à la Reich so it is also energized, works well.

As a witness or link to the original, use something that represents or symbolizes it: a photograph, a written name, a small figurine, a charm or even a coin. Change the numbers on the tuner by pasting new ones over the old ones. Relate the existing numbers to your rate sheet. If you decide to leave the batteries in the radio, be sure to use the earphone to reduce the sound when you turn the volume up. Since electricity is not necessary for a radionics machine, you might want to put one or more crystals in the battery chamber and connect them to the battery terminals.

When all is ready, turn the mode switch to AM ("Awareness Mode") and turn on the radio. Focus on the witness and slowly turn up the volume while rubbing the detector until you get a yes (sticky) response, telling you that you have amplified the input enough. Then focus on a question and slowly turn the tuner and rub the detector until you get another yes response. Check the tuner against your rate sheet and adjust as necessary. Continue to check the volume and use the tuner for each question that you ask.

2. *The Radionics Computer.* My terminology is oriented toward a Macintosh computer, so if you have another kind of computer, make adjustments as necessary.

Use a desktop publishing program to set up a full-page, horizontally or vertically as you prefer. Draw squares or circles with heavy lines to represent the input device, the amplifier, the tuner and the output device for use later. For a detector plate you can use the top of your keyboard or hard drive, or the side of your computer (Unmouse works well, too). You can title the drawings and connect them by "wires." Put a text block at one side for a rate sheet and one at the bottom to record your answers. This is your template or master sheet and you work only with a copy. In a scrapbook store various power symbols that you have drawn or scanned (crosses, spirals, stars, etc.) and number them. You might want to make them of increasing complexity or energy. Also store the various

rate sheets you intend to use and corresponding sets of
numbers for your tuner drawing. These numbers can
be horizontal or vertical. Your devices can be modified
into any shape you want.

To operate your radionics computer, put a text block
inside the input "device" and type in a name or a
description of what you want to investigate. Next
choose your rate sheet and paste it in the rate sheet
text block. Paste the corresponding numbers in the
tuner. Then ask for the most appropriate amplifier
symbol to use and rub until you get an answer. Paste it
in your amplifier device. Now focus on your specific
question and rub with one hand while you move your
mouse arrow to each number in your tuner device.
Record answers as you go. When you have finished,
either close without saving or save with a name in case
you want to work on that particular person or thing
again.

## Answers

Because you are working through the energies of the
earth, you can ask anything about anything. The
accuracy of the answers will depend on your energy
level, your ability to concentrate, your confidence, the
nature of your questions and the assumptions behind
your questions. If you assume that the Western model
of health and illness is correct, then your questions
about health and illness will reflect that view, and you
will get answers within that framework. If you assume
that certain behavioral symptoms are signs of the
presence of angels or demons, then your questions and
answers will reflect that framework. In other words,
your answers may or may not indicate objective facts
that are shared by most other people. It depends on
whether your assumptions are also shared.

# 7
# Psychotronics: Transmission at a Distance

"Psychotronics" is a term invented by Czech researchers as a replacement for "parapsychology," a term they felt was too closely associated with the occult. I borrow the term and apply it to the active *transmission* of *vril* through the use of various tools and devices, in contrast to the passive use discussed in the last chapter.

Mesmer used magnets to transmit *vril* to his patients, Reichenbach used long wires to bring *vril* from the sun to sensitives sitting in dark rooms. Reich used an "orgone shooter," a hand-held *vril* generator, to beam *vril* to specific parts of his patients' bodies. Hieronymous energized seeds in a dark basement by using wires leading to plates exposed to sunlight. A gentleman named Eemans strung wires between a healthy person's spine and an ill person's spine and clearly showed that healing energy traveled from one to the other.

In all the above examples a physical medium was used for the transmission of *vril*. This chapter describes a far stranger phenomenon: the transmission of *vril* at a distance without any visible medium at all.

## Cameron's Ray Gun

In Chapter 5 a beam of energy emitted upward from the tip of pyramids is described. Verne Cameron experimented a great deal with this feature in pyramids, cones and coils. To test the effect further, he invented a "ray gun" designed to focus the beam. This consisted of an 18-inch glass fluorescent tube, ¾" in diameter, with a ⅜" iron pipe placed inside. The outside of the glass was wound with copper wire. Cameron specified that a right-hand spiral was necessary with a cone and a left-hand spiral with a pyramid. Otherwise, he said, the beam would project through the handle instead of through the muzzle. The handle end was attached by a wire to the tip of the pyramid or cone. Cameron claimed to have found that the size of the wire made no difference. Using a 22-inch diameter cone attached to a ray gun, he projected the focused beam toward a building four miles away. Testing the beam with his Aurameter, he discovered that the force against the building was just as strong as it was on closer objects.

I tested a similar ray gun attached to an aluminum pyramid and felt a relatively mild energy transmission from the muzzle. As an experiment I built an 18x Manacube (akin to a 3x orac) and placed an electrode in the center with the wire from it attached to the gun. The energy emission was dramatically increased.

In testing further, I obtained a carbon rod of the type used for anodizing, ¾" in diameter and about a foot long. By itself the rod had an energy field (determined by dowsing) two to three inches wide along its entire length. Seven subjects were used for the test series. Six of these had previously reported that they could feel energy emission from the tip of a pyramid or from a Manabox. The seventh could not.

I shaped a rod into a flat-topped cone. Right-handed subjects held it in the left hand and left-handed subjects in the right hand. This was found to be the most effective arrangement. Six subjects reported that they could distinctly feel a beam of energy being emitted from the end of the rod. The one who had not felt anything from a pyramid tip felt nothing in this test. Strangely, when this subject held the cone, no emission could be felt by the others. In fact, the surrounding energy field seemed to have disappeared. It was as if she were absorbing all the energy. Others reported feeling the beam as far as ten feet away from the person holding the cone.

When the experimenter held the carbon rod in his left hand and placed his right hand on a 3x Manaplate, each of the six subjects reported that the beam suddenly increased in intensity and width. A measurement test with an Aurameter showed that, when the experimenter held the rod alone, the beam measured several inches in diameter, but when his other hand was placed on an 18x Manacube, the size of the emission jumped to a powerful four feet in diameter. However, while the sensitive subjects indicated that they felt the beam to be stronger, they perceived it as much narrower than four feet.

## The Signature Effect

In Los Angeles a company called E.S.P. Laboratory used to put out a product called a "thoughtform incubator," which was really just a cardboard pyramid. But according to the directions, if you placed your signature on a piece of paper, along with an expressed wish, at the center of the pyramid and chanted over it for several days, the desire would become manifest through sympathetic vibrations and the power of the pyramid. Certainly it would be easy to attribute results to the power of suggestion, but a number of reported effects led me to investigate the matter more closely.

I based my study on the theory that a signature, like a photograph, is linked to the person it came from through a universal field that can be activated and energized by *vril*. I began a series of tests to see whether something might actually be transferred to a person through a link placed in a pyramid. My first series of experiments indicated that this was so. When the signature of a subject was placed at the phi point in a pyramid, the subject reported that he or she could feel an influx of energy "coming from somewhere."

The next series of tests involved Manaboxes and were more controlled. Many subjects of all ages and both sexes were used. Subjects signed a piece of paper, laid it on a table, and then moved into another room where they sat quietly. The experimenter could observe them but they could not see what the experimenter was doing. The experimenter then alternately placed the subject's signature on the Manabox and took it away. Time and time again, the subject reported sensations of light, tingling or current while the signature was on the box and the disappearance of these sensations when it was removed. For most, it had a pleasant, energizing/calming effect. As an additional check, I had a clairvoyant observe the subjects during the test. As soon as the signature was placed on the box, she reported that the subject's aura increased in brightness and extent. Stronger Manaplates were used in the next test of this type, and I determined that an increase in the energy source increased the effects. In other tests, fatigued and depressed subjects regained energy and optimism moments after their signature was placed on a box or plate.

Eventually, it was found that if the signature was left on the box for several days without any further notice, the effects wore off to insignificance. Removing the signature for several more days and then replacing it resulted in the original sensations recurring. I can think of three explanations: the body reaches a saturation point of energy absorption and tunes out any further flow; or conscious attention plays an important role in energy effects; and/or energy sensations are like our sense of smell, in that continued stimulation causes desensitivity.

## Sound Transmission of *Vril*

Baron von Reichenbach did a series of experiments that suggested sound waves are another source of *vril*. With a sensitive in his dark room, Reichenbach struck pieces of metal and magnets together. The sensitive subjects reported that they immediately became luminous. A metal bell "shone so intensely, that a bright lustre pervaded the whole room, being seen by every sensitive person present." When a violin was played, both strings and sounding board became radiant and seemed to be surrounded by an aura. The higher the tone, the brighter the light. The sensitives placed their hands inside glass and metal bells without touching the sides. When the bells were struck, everyone reported feeling coolness against the left hand and warmth against the right, exactly the same types of sensations reported from other sources.

This experiment is extremely interesting in the light of the great respect paid to certain sounds by ancient cultures and esoteric groups. Pythagoras taught that sound is a creative force, and the therapeutic benefits of music have been extolled throughout the ages. Certain notes and sound patterns like "RA" and

"AUM" are thought to be especially beneficial. Experiments show that certain plants grow poorly when hard rock music is constantly played in their environment, but that they grow luxuriously to the sounds of most classical and religious music. According to Laurel Elizabeth Keyes, author of *Toning: The Creative Power of the Voice,* in their rituals Chinese healers struck flat pieces of jade that gave off healing vibrations. Mrs. Keyes developed a system of expressing sounds at different pitches to do healing at a distance. Apparently, the practitioner concentrates on the person to be healed while intoning the syllables. She reports excellent results.

In the field of psychotronics, Dr. Bhattacharyyan invented a device consisting mainly of a radio loudspeaker set to vibrate 120 cycles per second. This frequency is necessary, according to the inventor, to overcome the natural resistance in the aura of the individual and to allow the healing vibrations to enter. To carry out a long distance treatment, slips of paper with the patient's signature are hung in front of the loudspeaker while it vibrates. In more advanced work, specific jewels, each of which is supposed to have a particular healing potential, are hung in front of the loudspeaker along with the signatures.

It might be interesting to experiment in a similar way with the signature placed on the loudspeaker of a cassette player. A dowsing device or a radionics machine could be used to determine what piece of music has the most beneficial effect on a person, how long it should be played, and at what volume. If this works at all, I think you might find in general that music with a regular beat and structure would be good for people who need more stability and order in their lives. Airy new age music might benefit people who are too rigid in body or mind.

## A Psychotronics Pioneer

A pioneer in psychotronic transmission was Dr. Albert Abrams, at one time director of medical studies at Stanford University. While studying medicine in Europe, he had experiences that led him to the idea of using natural radiation fields for the diagnosis and treatment of disease. The traditional method of diagnosing used by Abrams is percussion, that is, tapping an area on the body and interpreting the resonance or dullness of the effect. Once, while tapping a patient, Abrams noted that the sound was dulled when a nearby X-ray machine was turned on if the patient was facing east-west, but the machine caused no effect when the man was aligned north-south. Abrams soon found that the same thing happened with a diseased person without a machine around. In other words, if a person with cancer or tuberculosis faced north, the tapping would produce a hollow resonance, which would become dull when the person faced east or west. A healthy person, on the other hand, would have a clear resonance in whatever direction he or she faced.

This phenomenon seemed to Abrams to be directly related to electromagnetism. If a large loop of wire connected to a galvanometer is held in a vertical plane oriented north-south, there is no reaction because the magnetic lines of the earth pass on either side of it. But if the loop is suddenly turned so that its plane is east-west, an electric current is induced. Experiments in which electrodes were attached to a salamander floating in a dish of water proved that this can happen in living organisms. As the salamander was rotated, an electric current was induced in this way. Perhaps this explains the power-building effects achieved by Middle Eastern and Indian dervishes and European witches

who claim to reach higher states of consciousness by
spinning rapidly in one spot.

Abrams devised experiments in which a healthy
subject facing west had specimens of diseased tissue
placed in contact with various parts of his body. These
areas were tapped and the differences in resonance
noted. Gradually, Abrams developed a theory that
disease is due to inharmonious vibrations which interfere with the natural vibratory harmony of the body.
He held that the efficacy of medicines was not due to
chemical action, but to the fact that they emit vibratory
radiations that cancel out the disease vibrations.

Prior to this, in addition to the tapping, Abrams had
rubbed a glass or rubber wand charged with static
electricity over subjects' abdomens. The wand was
retarded in its progress when a diseased organ was
present, as if a strong radiating field was being emitted.
(This sounds somewhat like Reich's findings with static
electricity, which he believed to be the same as orgone.)
It was not long before Abrams invented an electronic
device for detecting and interpreting the disease vibrations. His diagnostic machine, called a "Reflexophone,"
consisted mainly of a continuously variable resistor.
The machine was connected to the patient by electrodes and emitted sounds that replaced the need for
percussion or rubbing with a wand. Specific diseases
could be diagnosed by various rheostat settings.

The procedure originally used was to have the subject
stand facing west on a metal plate connected to a
ground. The plate was aluminum, as were the electrodes attached to the subject, but the wires were
copper. The grounding was apparently to reduce the
interference from surrounding electronic vibrations.
First, a system of spinal reflex concussion (tapping)
was used to dilate the diseased organ. Then the
electrodes were attached, one to the diseased area and

the other to the forehead or a point on the spine. With the use of the Reflexophone, the disease was then diagnosed.

Abrams made a leap forward when he discovered that he could diagnose any diseased condition and to what stage it had advanced, from a drop of the patient's blood. He could do this when the patient was far distant. The next step, of course, was an instrument designed to emit the proper vibrations for cancelling out the disease radiations without the use of medicine. This was the "Oscilloclast," built with the help of a radio engineer. Connected to an electric light socket and containing three rheostats, the machine was intended to emit the proper vibrations for cancelling out the disease after the patient had received spinal reflex dilation. There is ample evidence that it was effective, but until his death in 1924 Abrams was viciously attacked by the American Medical Association and the scientific community.

### Later Research

Abrams's work stimulated a host of other researchers, including Hieronymous and De la Warr. Nearly thirty years after Abrams's death, his principles were applied in ways that far exceeded anything he envisioned. In 1951 two American engineers, Curtis Upton and William Knuth, built an Abrams-type device to use on crop pests. Their innovation was the substitution of a photograph, rather than direct samples of the pests. The photograph was treated with an insecticide and the dials of the machine were set. Pests were eliminated on four thousand acres of cotton land. The same kind of instrument was used in another test on Japanese beetles that infested a cornfield. The area was rid of 80-90 percent of the beetles after a few five to ten minute

treatments, *except* for one small area that remained
100 percent infested. That area had been cut out of the
photograph used as the link. A company was formed
and psychotronic control of pests was begun on a large
scale through contracts with farmers. However, a combination of narrow-minded scientists, scared insecticide
companies and the USDA succeeded in forcing the
company to close down.

The Hieronymous Machine, a complicated adaptation
of the Abrams box, also was used to destroy pests. In
one instance, a man in New York with a tent cater-
pillar problem wrote to Hieronymous, who was in
Pennsylvania at the time, asking him to treat his cherry
tree. To the man's surprise, Hieronymous merely asked
for a photo of the tree, the negative and a few leaves
and caterpillars. A few days later, the man arrived
home to find all the caterpillars that were in his tree
lying in a circle on the ground, stone dead. Apparently,
they had been killed from three hundred miles away!

In another experiment, Hieronymous used his device
to treat three ears of corn, each inhabited by a corn
worm. After treating the corn ten minutes per hour on
a twenty-four hour basis for three days, two of the
worms were reduced to mush, but the third was still
functioning. After another twenty-four hours of treatment it, too, was mush, and the first two were only
"wet places" on the ears of corn.

This profoundly affected Hieronymous, who vowed to
reveal the full secrets of his invention only to those he
was sure would never misuse it. He was not the only
one so affected. The implications shook John Campbell
so much that he wrote Hieronymous, saying that the
findings implied it was possible to kill a person with
such a machine despite all one might do to hide and
without having any chance to protect or defend oneself
against the attack. Campbell further stated that the

Hieronymous Machine was like actual magic, in that it could, in a sense, cast spells of death or life through the laws of sympathetic magic, as has been demonstrated by sorcerers all over the world.

## Natural Protection from Transmission of Harm

Huna theory throws light on the idea of sending death or healing from a distance. It is commonly supposed in the West that suggestion is operating when someone is affected at a distance for good or ill. That is, the subject of the "spell" must know what is intended and believe in the power of the spell-caster. His or her subconscious works on the suggestion and turns it into a physical experience. While this technique is often used, it is not necessary for those who know the right procedure. There is ample proof in the literature that the recipient does not have to know anything at all about what is happening. I am personally familiar with cases in Africa and Hawaii where this type of operation was carried out, both for beneficial and for destructive ends.

However, human beings are not worms. We have far greater egos, or, if you prefer, a far greater degree of self-awareness and self-determination, as well as much higher levels of energy. Thought or psychotronic transmissions with intent to harm are rarely effective with humans because they are counter to our natural urge for survival. Therefore such transmissions require not only tremendous levels of energy and concentration, but a recipient with very low self-esteem and intense fear or guilt. This may be why sorcerers the world over go out of their way to make sure their victims know they are under attack, and why they always have poisons or weapons ready in case the spell does not work.

On the other hand, thought or psychotronic transmission with the intent to heal or help is almost always effective to some degree because it reinforces our urge toward survival and our natural desires to be healthy, wealthy, happy and successful. Unfortunately, the type of person described above as most susceptible to harm is the least susceptible to help, and high energy and concentration may be necessary to break through the inhibitions of fear, guilt and/or low self-esteem.

## The Power of Thought

George De la Warr continued research from where Abrams had left off, and without knowing anything about the work of Hieronymous or Keith and Upton, he confirmed several of their findings. For instance, he found that energy could be focused through a lens, as did Hieronymous, Mesmer and Reichenbach. And he discovered for himself that the energy could be transmitted through a photograph. This is how he successfully treated diseased and undernourished plants. In a unique series of experiments, De la Warr prepared two soil plots of completely homogeneous makeup. One plot was treated by photograph for a month with energy patterns equivalent to plant nutrients. The other was left alone. Four young cabbages were then planted in each site. For the first two weeks no difference in growth was noticeable, but by the end of three months the cabbages in the treated soil had grown three times larger than the controls.

De la Warr next tested broccoli planted in treated soil and controls separated by a buffer zone. Photographs were taken of the plants and treatment was given daily for six months. The average increase in crop yield from the treated plants as compared to the controls was 81 percent. A further test on beans in a plot two miles away produced similar results, and a test on a plot in

Scotland carried out from Oxford was another success, yielding carrots 20 percent heavier than nontreated ones.

Could the energy be stored in an inert substance to be released elsewhere over a period of time? De la Warr tested this idea by treating vermiculite and then mixing it with seeds and planting them together. Yield increases over controls were up to 270 percent.

Up to this point De la Warr was not certain how the energy worked to increase plant growth, but a drastic failure led him to the explanation. A national plant-breeding organization requested some of the vermiculite to test. They got none of the results reported by De la Warr. However, when De la Warr himself went to their laboratory and carried out the tests, results were the same as before. This led De la Warr to realize that the human mind is the most vital factor. To test this concept he had assistants prepare some tests with vermiculite, telling them what part was treated and what was untreated. In fact, none of the vermiculite had been treated. Nevertheless, the plants that the assistants *thought* were treated grew faster than the others.

Many more experiments have shown the importance of thought in this process. Two famous psychics, Ambrose and Olga Worrall, were asked by a scientist to concentrate on rye seedlings six hundred miles from their home. Carefully controlled, the test showed that the seedlings immediately responded to the thoughts and within twelve hours were growing at a rate 84 percent faster than normal. In other tests carried out in France, the growth of fungus was retarded by nearly 100 percent by thought alone. At U.C.L.A., Olga Worrall was invited to test her healing ability on a plant. To her dismay, it soon wilted and died. Quite upset, she asked to come back and try again. This time her treated plant thrived. Her opinion was that she had used too much energy the first time.

I inadvertently confirmed this interpretation even before I heard of the Worrall test. In my home I had a rubber tree which had been taken as a cutting from a larger plant. Though green and with healthy leaves, it had not grown at all in over a month. I poured as much energy into it as I could for half an hour. The next day the tip of the plant began to wither. On the second day the leaves all fell off and the top third of the plant was brown and wrinkled. By the third day the whole plant looked like someone had set a blowtorch to it. The result was similar to an experience of Reich's in which an overdose of energy caused all the trees around his laboratory in Maine to turn brown. However, what constitutes an overdose depends on the size, structure and energy capacity of the recipient. Humans can easily handle energy levels that would wither plants, and some humans can handle much more energy than others.

Thought is vital, but so is *vril*. We come back to the theory that results like these are the effect of *aka*, the etheric field, being altered or influenced by *vril*, which has been stimulated or directed by thought.

## The Czech Connection

The main character in this section is Robert Pavlita, a Czechoslovakian metallurgist who worked for many years on his version of psychotronic generators. These are metal alloys in various shapes and sizes that are designed to receive a charge of energy from the human body (or mind) and then transmit that energy to perform specific functions. Working with alloys, Pavlita discovered a substance that would attract nonmagnetic particles after he had handled it for awhile. At first he was convinced that the metal somehow accumulated static electricity, but he had to lay this idea aside when his alloy began attracting nonmagnetic particles under water, which static electricity cannot do. Furthermore, the objects attracted could then attract other objects. According to Pavlita, the original inspiration for his devices came from an ancient manuscript, probably one dealing in alchemy.

Most of the information available to the general public on Pavlita's work comes from the book *Psychic Discoveries Behind the Iron Curtain,* by Sheila Ostrander and Lynn Schroeder. On a reporting trip to eastern Europe they viewed films of the psychotronic generators, had a personal demonstration by Pavlita and operated a device themselves.

The device that first astounded the Czech scientific world was a small bit of metal, previously charged by Pavlita, sealed into a metal box, with a motor that turned an armature sticking out the top. The bit of metal was not connected to anything. On top of the armature sat a strip of copper. When the motor was started, the copper strip turned with the armature. The amazing part is that when Pavlita stared hard at the box containing his generator, the copper strip soon stopped and began turning in the direction opposite to the rotating shaft. It sounds like psychokinesis, the ability to move external objects with the mind. But Pavlita insisted he was merely a technologist working through a tool with a natural energy.

Other generators have been used to turn blades and even motors, according to the Czechs, which again reminds one of Reich. Like the treatments from the De la Warr machine, some of Pavlita's generators apparently irradiate seeds so that they grow larger and faster than untreated seeds. More and more it becomes evident that Pavlita found another way to generate and transmit *vril*. He had one construction in the shape of a doughnut with a slice cut out of one side. Flies placed in the center died immediately. This is reminiscent of my own experience with roaches, and of course the pest control by Hieronymous and the two engineers. Still other devices had the appearance of abstract metal sculptures with curious knobs and indentations and "staring patterns."

The staring patterns are said to be a means of aiding concentration for the purpose of charging or releasing the energy in the generators. In some cases, Pavlita charged a generator by handling it or placing it to his temple. Then he stared at it to release and direct the energy. Some odd facts discovered by Vern Cameron may have a bearing here. While outlining the human energy field with his Aurameter, Cameron found that particularly strong beams of energy were emitted from the left temple and the left eye. He felt that they had something to do with telepathy. It may be that they are involved with *vril* transmission, too. The Czech experimenters say that no special thought need be held while charging a generator or releasing the energy. I find this hard to accept, as it goes contrary to my experience and knowledge. True, everything handled absorbs some personal energy, and staring alone will transmit some *vril*. But I feel something else is going on that has not been said. Perhaps a mental state of expectation rather than a specific mental image is held. Or perhaps the alloyed devices are *vril* generators like crystals, so that instead of charging them, Pavlita himself is being charged, making his energy transmission through staring more powerful.

Ostrander and Schroeder were handed a wooden stick at one point that had been prepared under pressure by a special process and charged to channel a person's "biological" energy. They were able to attract and pick up pieces of crystal and metal with it, as if it were a strange kind of magnet. It was supposed to work under water as well. They were told it did not work as well when one is tired. Other generators were said to speed the healing process, as some of my own generators appear to do, and still others caused changes in EEG readings and spatial disorientation when directed at a person.

On a visit to Pavlita's home, Ostrander and Schroeder were shown a small but heavy trapezoidal device with an attachment on top that could be changed for different purposes. Pavlita charged it by touching projections on the front and back and staring at it in a certain pattern that was engraved into the device. Another device was a copper collar about five inches high and ten inches in diameter, with an inch-wide gap in the side. At one edge of the collar was the generator, a small tube of metal. On this, Pavlita placed a metal ball. Then, from behind a plate of glass, he and his daughter began the staring pattern. A tin wheel was mounted in the center of the collar on a spike. In a few moments it began to turn. A Czech scientist who was present said that the copper seemed to attract the energy and that the collar seemed to polarize it. Another way to do this is described at the end of this chapter.

Very interesting, too, was another demonstration in which metal filings were scattered on a plate of glass, under which was placed a powerful horseshoe magnet. A tubular generator of steel with an aluminum tip was held over the filings, and it easily picked them up, in spite of the attractive force of the magnet. The same generator also picked up nonmagnetic items.

Some of Pavlita's generators functioned as ESP devices. One had a rotating pointer on top. Below the pointer, ESP cards were arranged in a circle. The "sender" in another room had another deck, which was shuffled for random distribution. He then picked a card and concentrated on its pattern. In the next room, the pointer turned to the correct card in the circle. The rate of accuracy was said to be 100 percent. The generator was said to be able to pick out other objects as well and to distinguish blood samples.

A statement of Pavlita's seems to support the huna theory: "Every motion a person makes in a room leaves a pattern, a trace." Another Czech experimenter added that the trace is a sort of indentation of form made in the surroundings. A generator linked through the *aka* field to a person in another room could respond to that person's concentrated thought, *if* the generator could be made to release the thought energy when it received the thought impulse. We know how to establish the psychic bond, and we know how to charge an object with *vril*. What Pavlita knows and we do not is how to cause that energy to be released in a specific way. This is the real mystery of Pavlita's work.

A few Czech statements give tantalizing clues to the mystery. "The *mind* seems to control this energy." We know this, but perhaps Pavlita is doing something we do not know about with his mind. "The secret of the generators is in their *form* . . . it's their shape that lets you accumulate this energy and turn it to whatever purpose you want." This reminds one of the pyramid. It may be that we already have the shapes, but we do not know how to apply them properly. The shapes used by Pavlita are extremely varied, yet simple. "It's the juxtaposition of materials within a specific form that makes it work." We know something about these ideas. Pyramids depend on form, and oracs depend on juxtaposition of materials. Pyramids built with orac-type layers are much more powerful than simple pyramids. The energy field is changed when this is done, but we do not know exactly how, nor what uses for it might be

possible. The energy field is also changed in a pyramid
when it is truncated, but we are still searching for
applications. All shapes seem to create specific energy
patterns, and all materials have specific energy fields.
We will have to piece together these bits of knowledge
by stimulating our ingenuity and intuition to the limit. In
the process, it is quite possible that we will come up
with ideas that make our present efforts seem like child's
play in comparison.

### Personal Experiments

You can turn your radionics machine into a
psychotronic transmitter very easily. You'll recall
mention of an output device for the radionics radio.
This would most reasonably be the speaker. When
transmitting, move the witness/link to the speaker (on
top or in front). Then, using a rate sheet for remedies
based on your diagnosis, place the stick plate at the
antenna (input) to pick the appropriate remedy. With
the help of the stick plate you can also adjust the
volume (amplification) and length of time for treatment.

For remedies, you could use flower essences, per-
fumes, over-the-counter medicines, crystals, or whatever. Remember, you are "sending" only the *idea
pattern* of the remedy, not the remedy itself. If your
radio contains an audio cassette player, or if you can
attach one, then you can also use music as a remedy,
setting your witness/link right on top of or in front of
the music being played, à la Bhattacharyyan. For the
radionics computer, you can do essentially the same,
cutting and pasting the witness/link into the output
section and pasting a remedy symbol into the input
section for the time duration chosen. Since mental
focus is always a vital part of the operation, it is best to
intentionally focus, by using an image or sense of

expectation, for at least one minute for any operation. Then leave the remedy "turned on" without personal attention for the rest of the time allotted.

I first ran across a simple device, somewhat resembling one of Pavlita's psychotronic generators, in a book by Claude Bristol called *The Magic of Believing*. Since then I have demonstrated it at many workshops and even once on television, and I have taught many others how to use it.

The simplest form of it is made from a paper cup (not the cone-shaped kind), a push pin and a piece of paper about three inches square. Make sure that your environment is free of air movement, including stray breezes from doors and windows. On the floor or on a table in front of you, turn the cup upside down and place the push pin point up on top of it. Fold the paper square corner to corner, and then open it up so it has a flattened tent shape. Place the center of the paper on the pin so that it balances without touching the cup. Then cup your hands around the paper and watch what happens.

For most people the paper turns a little right away. For some it begins to spin, and for some it does not move at all at first. Experiment by moving your hands, using imagination and/or will, getting emotional, being neutral and anything else you can think of. With practice you will be able to turn the paper at will, even getting it to change direction when you want.

You will have no doubt that the paper is moving in response to your energy and your mind. You might try handling the cup, pin and paper beforehand, "charging" them at your forehead or temple, to see if that makes a difference. Sometimes I get better effects by deep breathing and exercising beforehand, and once, in a high emotional state, I was able to get results through a sealed glass container.

# 8
# Vivaxis: Attuning to the Earth's Energies

Sometime in the early 1960s a woman named Frances Nixon, while working with healing energies, made a discovery that led to a novel method of healing and attuning oneself to the natural magnetic energies of the earth. She also discovered some fascinating and unusual ways of producing *vril* which I have verified.

The term "vivaxis" could be translated as "life axis." Its meaning will become clearer as I summarize Nixon's work. First, she contended that the atoms and molecules in our bones become permanently aligned at the time of birth or shortly before. This alignment is magnetic and takes on the characteristic pattern of the geographical point of birth. It is a scientific fact that molten metals or rocks realign their atomic structure in accordance with the prevailing magnetic field as they solidify. This is probably where Nixon got her idea. No doubt she chose bones because they are the most solid part of the body.

While quite flexible for several weeks before birth, the bones are still pretty solid, and the cells of bones are renewed throughout life. One would think that new cells would take on the magnetic characteristics prevailing at the point where they were formed. For many

**155**

people this would vary frequently. I am inclined therefore to be skeptical of Nixon's conclusion that the
bones are involved in a special alignment. However,
I believe that the body retains a strong memory of
the prevailing energy patterns at the highly charged
moment of birth. However, this minor question regarding alignment does not affect the validity of the rest
of Nixon's findings.

## The Personal Vivaxis

Because of the alignment of bone cells, whether actual
or remembered, Nixon believed it was possible to
locate the direction of the place where a person was
born, as well as its altitude, in relation to the point of
search. This is possible because all people are supposed
to be linked by "wave circuits" to the magnetic field of
their birthplace, which is called the "vivaxis." In huna
terms, it would seem that the link is through the *aka*
field. Nixon goes on to say that by "channeling" (aligning) oneself in the direction of the birthplace, a person
can be put in phase with the vivaxis with healthful
results, sometimes of a startling nature. This phasing is
supposed to be done by means of "particle currents,"
which run side by side in opposite directions. Frankly,
I do not understand this idea.

Not only is channeling (described later in more detail)
supposed to strengthen one's own field in a healthy
way, but it can be used to destroy foreign energy fields
such as those of bacteria and viruses. This resembles
Abrams's concept, only without the help of electronics.
According to Nixon, the thyroid gland and blood
record the alignment to the vivaxis in some fashion not
made clear. She believed that cigarette tobacco and
insecticides weaken and disrupt the alignment. (She
also believed that the geographic location where a bar

magnet was magnetized could be pinpointed.)

A major point in Nixon's early research was that the most effective healing came from a person's own magnetic energies when properly adjusted. Energy from other sources, such as magnets, could provide temporary relief. But such foreign energy might actually prove harmful in the long run and the body would reject it unless it were strong enough to cause a complete realignment of the whole body energy field. Therefore, proper channeling became one of her most important techniques.

## Channeling

The technique of channeling is carried out with the help of two dowsing devices, one held in each hand. Pendulums have been used, but the preferred type is an 18″ soft steel rod ⅛″ in diameter, bent in the middle to form a right angle. One end of the rod is placed in a 6″ copper sleeve ¼″ in diameter. Both ends of the steel rod should be pointed, and the rod should be able to swing freely in the sleeve. This is very similar to a popular dowsing device called an "L" rod. Nixon's idea is that the steel temporarily becomes magnetized as it becomes properly aligned, and the copper conducts the energies.

The rods should be held well away from the body. The individual should take off glasses, jewelry and watches; loosen any tight clothing; stand on level ground or on cement, wood, blacktop or linoleum; and avoid deflections caused by the proximity of mountains, planes, electrical equipment, metal or fireglass roofs, overhead branches, people walking on the floor above, storms, spectators, etc. The alignment of the head is also important, for if it is turned a fraction to one side the wave pickup is weakened. In

addition, people who have had extensive X-rays, those
with blocked sinuses and those with disrupted finger
receptors (see below) will not be able to record the
energies. Actually, all of this suggests that the only way
to channel would be to be 100 percent healthy standing
stark naked in the middle of the Sahara with a wooden
neck brace. But Nixon recorded many instances in
which effective channeling was done under far less
than ideal conditions.

The dowsing rods should be marked for left and right
hands and always used in that way. They should be
used by only one person because they become "magnetized" and lose efficiency when used out of that
person's alignment. Once the individual is ready to
channel, she stands like a ramrod with feet well apart,
holding the dowsing rods out from the body at
about shoulder level. The direction to face may be
determined approximately with a compass. The
individual then turns stiffly by degrees until the two
rods cross in front of her. At this point, if everything
else is in order, she will be aligned in her channel.

There are other ways to use the rods. Another way to
determine the channel using only one rod is to hold it
in the right hand. Then position the middle finger of
the left hand at the level of the tip of the rod and
about four or five inches away from it. When correctly
aligned, the tip of the rod swings toward the middle
finger. A method for determining the channel when
one is out of alignment is to hold the rod in the right
hand and position the thumb of the left hand directly
under the tip of the rod. The rod swings in the
direction of the channel. Still another method is to use
one rod and concentrate on something like the multi-
plication tables. The rod automatically swings in the
direction of the vivaxis. There is a curious correspondence here as the same technique is used to produce

alpha waves. The rods are used only to find the
channel and are laid aside when the actual channeling
is done.

After the channel has been found, the process of
"channeling" begins with the individual standing in the
channel for about seven seconds while breathing
deeply. Then she turns clockwise and does the same
at 90 degree intervals until a full circle is made.
Then she reverses the procedure and moves counterclockwise for three more 90 degree stops. She then
stops and moves out of the alignment. Normally this
should not be done again for five or so days. Nixon
warned that channeling is highly stimulating and must
not be overdone. She also warned that other persons
ought not to watch the one who is channeling as they
become part of the circuit, and the channeled energies
might be detrimental to them.

What does it feel like when the channel is found? I
ran a test with a subject who seemed to fit the necessary qualifications. Using the methods outlined, he
apparently found his channel. He felt an immediate
flux of energy and a strong pull in the direction of the
vivaxis. Inadvertently, another individual was sitting
between him and the vivaxis, though not looking at
him. As soon as the subject aligned, this person
reported a sudden tingling sensation across her legs but
with no detrimental effects. In later experiments I had
classes of twenty or more people all locating their birth
vivaxis at the same time. Most felt some kind of
energizing, and we never had any ill effects.

### Neutralizing

According to Nixon, one should undergo a process
called "neutralizing" before channeling. The purpose of
neutralizing is to counteract an overcharge in the elec-

trical body field due to such things as major earthquakes, storms, magnetic disturbances and electrical or
electronic equipment. These create imbalanced conditions in which the body does not respond to channeling, and adverse conditions might even result. One
of the earlier methods used by Nixon was to place a
block of ice or a container of acid, such as vinegar or
vitamin C solution, between the ankles for ten minutes
to "ground out excess static." This was to be done
every day for four days prior to channeling. It was
important to sit out of the channel, with the head tilted
and the hands grounded on the thighs. If ice was used,
it had to be unchlorinated.

Fortunately, Nixon gave an alternative method that is
much less cumbersome and uncomfortable, which led
me to a large number of positive experiments. In this
method one stands inside a hoop of galvanized wire
about four feet in diameter for thirty seconds. Nixon
stated that this neutralizes or insulates the area inside
the hoop and a column of equivalent diameter above it.
The neutral field is supposed to absorb the static
charge of the person in the hoop. I and hundreds of
subjects experimented with galvanized hoops, copper
hoops, rope hoops and even plastic hula hoops. I do
not know whether any static charges were neutralized,
but I can say that the experience is refreshing, energizing, calming and healing, depending on the state of
the person. It does not seem to matter what material is
used. The sense of being in a column of energy is one
of the most frequently reported effects. Meditating in
a hoop is a delightful experience, also.

A third type of neutralization is called the "accordion
method." The fingers and thumbs of the two hands are
brought together, with a space between the palms.
Then the hands are pushed in and out like an accordion while one breathes deeply. Interestingly, I have

long taught this technique (without the accordion push) as a means of calming down clients who are nervous, excited or upset, or as a prelude to healing or meditating. It seems to have the effect of harmonizing one's personal field.

Nixon said that neutralizing the dowsing rods was also necessary to remove the field they received during manufacture. She recommended that they be held under running tap water and thoroughly immersed. Running water does neutralize static electricity; it does generate a field of negative (calming) ions; and it has long been used by healers to neutralize "bad vibrations." However, based on my own experience and shamanic teachings, I think neutralizing the rods is merely a placebo that might be useful for insecure people.

## Code Receptors

An essential part of Nixon's method is the stimulation of what she called "code receptors." These are points on the body, particularly the head, which are supposed to act as wave receptors for energies coming from both outside the body and from within it. Some of these, called "heart receptors," are supposedly stimulated when a person projects thoughts into the outer world. The receptors are centers of swirling energy normally attuned to the vivaxis field, but they can become unbalanced when subjected to X-rays, strong magnetic fields or electrotherapy. Such therapies can cause secondary or false vivaxes for parts of the body, while the rest responds to the original vivaxis. The resulting imbalance weakens the total field and allows the entrance of foreign energies from viruses and bacteria. Prior to channeling, the code receptors are stimulated by tapping, by hot water sprays or in other ways. The idea is that this puts them into a neutral state that enables the channeling to reorient them properly to the vivaxis.

It is not clear where Nixon got the idea of the code receptors, but it appears to be an independent discovery. It is interesting that they appear to be identical to acupuncture points.

Nixon believed that every time we concentrate on something in our environment, whether a person or an object, we tend to absorb some of its energy into our system through certain receptors and communication pathways between them. Normally, this does no harm since a multitude of foreign waves tend to cancel each other out. If we concentrate on another person or object for a long time, however, Nixon says we accumulate that radiation until it begins to upset our own system. She describes a person who had disturbed receptors leading to a tumor under one arm after being greatly concerned about a sick relative. On the other hand, she suggested that tuning into a person with a tranquil mind can be beneficial, because some of the tranquil energies are absorbed.

An ancient esoteric practice is to meditate on or contemplate a natural force, a hero or heroine, a god or a goddess, with such devotion that you begin to have the same qualities and powers as the object of your focus. From a huna and shamanic point of view, you are not absorbing the energies of the object. Instead you are mimicking its internal and external patterns that are being broadcast through the *aka* field, visibly or telepathically. The same thing occurs in a negative way if you focus on someone, not out of devotion, but from worry, anxiety, fear or anger. To help people break such a negative link, I have them first focus on some positive source of energy, strength, calm or beauty. Then they contemplate their former objects of fear or anger while imagining them surrounded by a field of harmonious energy that protects or harmonizes.

Nixon emphasized the need for "grounding" after prolonged mental contact with another person. The method she used was to press her hands on a table, supposedly because the table would absorb the foreign energies. But any of the neutralizing systems mentioned above also work. She said that the continual practice of "mentally channeling" into others is a violation of the laws of nature and might injure someone. But that is like saying that communicating by radio is against the laws of nature and might injure someone. Everyone (and everything) is continuously "broadcasting" everything about themselves on many different "frequencies" all the time. Most of us stumble onto one or more of these frequencies from time to time in ways that we call intuition or hunches. A few people have developed this natural human talent to a high degree. The act of tuning in cannot harm anyone; it is the message that matters.

According to Nixon, hypnosis has a definite effect on certain code receptors. It is as if a secondary alignment is established to the hypnotist or the place where one was hypnotized, indicating that a strong bond was made during the hypnotic process. To disrupt such a bond, Nixon advocated a technique of striking the code receptors in the center of the forehead and the back of the head with the heel of the hands, and then immediately channeling. Note the similarity between this and Abrams's technique of striking certain points on the spine just prior to irradiating the person with electrical energies.

As a former professional hypnotherapist, I believe that a bond such as Nixon described is not impossible, but it is certainly not usual, and it exists only in the mind of the person hypnotized. Hypnosis is nothing more than a form of guided meditation (and vice versa).

The hypnotist has no special power. He or she merely speaks or reads some words that suggest certain experiences. Another person hears those words and follows them to a greater or lesser degree. If the second person believes in the power of hypnosis strongly, then he or she tends to follow the suggestions more readily. The same is true if the hypnotist has a strong personality and/or an abundant charge of *vril*. Generally speaking, the best hypnotic subject is one who has a good imagination and who is either highly motivated or has low self-esteem.

Stimulating the code receptors by striking or tapping is the equivalent in acupuncture of inserting needles; in acupressure of pressing or massaging the same points; and in zone therapy (also called reflexology) of similarly stimulating points on the hands and feet. In Nixon's system the purpose is to disrupt the influence of foreign wave patterns so that the receptors can be tuned in through channeling to more beneficial radiations. In acupressure and zone therapy the purpose is to break up blocks in the body energy circuit so that energy imbalances can be restored to their proper equilibrium. With acupuncture it is partly the latter and also to introduce beneficial energies from the outside.

In the Hawaiian system of bodywork that I learned, the main energy centers are the joints plus the crown, brow, chest, navel, back of neck, base of spine, hands and feet. In times of emotional stress or physical stress (such as comes from sitting at a computer writing a book), personal *vril* seems to accumulate or get stuck at these points. I have found it very beneficial at such times to gently but rapidly tap these points (usually in a quick 5-beat or a 4-4-5-beat series) as a means of relaxing and recharging. On the floor in my office I have an energy device on which I stand from time to time in line with the magnetic field of the earth for additional recharging. A few moments ago I stopped writing, tapped my points, and immediately stood aligned on my floor device. I have to say that the effect is very stimulating, refreshing and lasting.

It may be that stimulation of various points on the body puts the bioenergy in a state of flux and ready to realign with the next strong energy field focused on or encountered. If this is the case, then a useful addition to acupuncture, acupressure, zone therapy or even massage would be a strong *vril* generator and/or compass in order to realign yourself with abundant and beneficial *vril*. Of course, you could also use Nixon's vivaxis concept if you choose.

### Creating Vivaxes

In one experiment Nixon created a vivaxis or an energy vortex with nothing more than a ballpoint pen. She placed a pad of unlined paper on a level surface previously determined to be neutral by means of a dowsing rod. A pendulum ought to do as well. She handled the paper only by the edges. Using a ruler, she rapidly drew a one-inch line with the pen, and without hesitation drew a second line as rapidly from the opposite direction so that they met exactly in the center without any overlap, forming a two-inch line. She waited thirty seconds to allow the energies to organize themselves. A check with a dowsing rod showed that an energy vortex was emitting from the center of the two-inch line. An entity—the line—had been born, and a vivaxis created. When the line was removed from its "birthplace," a test with a dowsing rod showed that a vivaxis remained on the table and that a link still existed between the vivaxis and the line on the paper. Friends and I have verified this effect many times, and I found that a nice vivaxis was created when four lines were drawn rapidly toward a center point, leaving them up to one inch apart.

## Salt and Soda

In a similar experiment Nixon purposely waited ten seconds before drawing the second part of the line. The result was a reaction over the center point similar to that over disturbed code receptors in a person. Two pupils whom she was training in her system, one a doctor, had been experimenting with ways to counteract the effects of radioactive fallout. They had experimented with immersing the body in a solution containing one pound of sea salt and one pound of baking soda. The effect on fallout is not known, but research by Nixon's followers suggested that such a bath had the effect of removing foreign wave interference, even of energies thought to be permanently superimposed on one's own pattern. The information gleaned from dowsing people after such a bath was corresponded with changes the dowser had interpreted as indicating removal of wave interference.

Nixon mixed equal parts of sea salt and soda in a plastic bag and set it for a few seconds on the "disturbed" line she had drawn. The energy balance was corrected and stayed corrected for fifteen minutes. When the compound was passed over a person's code receptors *without actually touching them,* it was found that the person's energy field automatically lined up with his or her vivaxis for the same period of time. Eventually it was found that the compound could be used only for a certain length of time. If used longer it apparently absorbed too much energy and became disturbed itself.

The next step was to test the salt and soda in separate containers to see whether there was any relationship between them. When placed in reasonable proximity, it was found that there was a definite exchange of energy between them. When aligned to the points of the compass, east-west or north-south, the energy flow was even stronger. The energy flow between the two, particularly in the east-west arrangement, also produced a vertical flow of energy extending both up and down from the center of the distance between them. Depending on time and place and possibly solar or lunar activity, the upward energy was found to be compatible with the body field, while the downward one was incompatible. Sometimes this occurred with the salt on the west and sometimes it had to be placed on the east. In the opposite arrangements at these times, the upward energy was incompatible and detrimental. To identify these forces Nixon coined the terms "arealoha" (meaning to her "are friendly") for the harmonious force and "non-aloha" for the inharmonious force. Exceptionally interesting is her observation that the compatible energy flow had a soft, cool texture, while the incompatible force felt unpleasant and sticky. Reichenbach's sensitives exploring the polarization of od reported exactly the same thing, an indication that Nixon's forces and *vril* are the same.

I have conducted quite a number of experiments with sea salt and soda. Like Nixon, I found that only sea salt works. Ordinary table salt is inert, perhaps because it has already absorbed too much from other sources. In an experiment using seven subjects, I placed one-half cup each of sea salt and soda in glass jars with metal lids. I put them on a table eight inches apart, with the salt west of the soda. Tests were carried both by hand and with sensitive pendulums. Only one subject was familiar with Nixon's work.

In the first round of testing, the subjects placed a

hand, usually the left, between the jars and moved it
around to check effects. The subjects did not reveal
their sensations until after the testing to avoid the
possibility of suggestion. Subject 1 felt irregular pricks
of current in his hand and on his face. There also
seemed to be a kind of magnetic pull downward near
the table and a focal point of energy about six to eight
inches above the level of the tops of the jars. Subject 2
felt a cool sensation in a certain spot. This is one who
normally felt warmth from Manaboxes and pyramids.
Subject 3 experienced a "warmish" feel at first, and felt
a focal point above the jars as well as a magnetic pull
near the table. She also felt a tingle up the arm and
said the energy increased with time. Subject 4 felt a
warmish energy field "like a ball of black velvet."
Subject 5 felt a current running up her arm when her
hand was near the table and at a focal point above.
Subject 6 felt tingling and a cool sensation, a focus at
eight inches above the jars, and a magnetic pull downward. Subject 7 felt a downward pull at the level of the
contents and at a focal point above the jars. Gradually,
all determined that there was an "energy bridge" between the jars approximately 1″x1″ in diameter at the
level of the contents.

With the salt east of the soda there was a difference.
The "bridge" was still there, and there were prickly
currents. All felt a thick, mushy field near the base of
the contents, similar to what Nixon described as "incompatible." Subject 1 thought the effect was unpleasant, but Subject 3 did not think so. The others did not
make a judgment. Sensitives observing the auras of the
subjects reported that when the salt was west and a
hand between the jars, the aura tended to increase in
size and brightness. But with the salt east it was
reduced both in size and brightness.

Pendulum testing with the salt west showed an

extensive force field around the jars, extending at least two feet. Closer in, the pendulum seemed drawn in from the south, and the "bridge" acted as a channel in which the pendulum swung freely. On the north side, a strong field swung out in an arc. The focal point above the field could not be determined with the pendulum, and the supposition is that it must be very narrow. As the pendulum was swung slowly through the bridge, three subjects reported seeing a distinct "auric wake."

Later, Subject 4 bent down from the south and put his head between the jars with no noticeable effect. Subjects 1 and 2 did the same, and both felt a flush of blood in the face. Then Subject 4 did the same from the north and immediately got a terrible headache. This disappeared, however, when he put his head back in from the south. No one cared to repeat his experiment. Nixon had advised never placing the head between the two elements.

In another experiment on a different date, only two subjects participated. This time the jars were laid on their sides with the metal caps pointing to each other. The field between them was reported to be very cool and of cylindrical shape, the size of the caps. The aura was said to brighten considerably when a hand was placed within the field. With the salt west the feeling was comfortable, but with salt east it was uncomfortable. When the jars were placed north-south, the field could not be felt at all. This confirms Abrams's reactions and Reich's contention that atmospheric orgone flows from west to east.

During the same experimental series, one-half cup of sea water was placed four inches to the west of one tablespoon of soda dissolved in half a cup of water. The forefinger of the left hand was dipped in the sea water and the forefinger of the right hand was dipped in the soda solution. The aura was seen to increase

greatly in size and brightness, and each subject felt
the influx of a sense of well-being that lasted after the
fingers were removed. Then each container was placed
on a Manabox with eight inches between them, and the
procedure was repeated. The effects were as before,
only much more intense. Then the jars of salt and soda
were placed upright on the Manaboxes and a hand was
placed on each with the same glow of body and aura.
With or without the Manaboxes, the hands on top of the
jars produced a good effect when the salt was west, but
when the salt was placed east the body felt drained of
energy.

As far as I can determine, the sea salt is an energy
source and acts as the transmitter, with soda being
neutral but acting as a receiver when put in circuit
with the salt. A curious fact is that salt and sea water
have been used all around the world for millennia as a
means of exorcising evil spirits and restoring health.
When Nixon said that the arealoha energies possess the
power to erase foreign influences and increase one's
resistance by fortifying the energy circuit, she is saying
the same thing in different words and based on a
different set of beliefs.

This agreement should encourage us to look at past
practices in a new light. Much of what was done in the
past is valid, even though we may not agree with the
premises on which the practices were based.

## Nixon's Recommendations

Nixon warned us to avoid absorbing non-aloha forces,
as subject 4 apparently did when he placed his head
between the jars. Also, one has to avoid absorbing the
"unsorted ambient forces." This is a little harder to
understand. Nixon had an idea that certain wave
vectors flow upward at angles, and these are harmful if

absorbed. These vectors occur from the north, so she recommended that the fingers of the hand always be pointed toward the south when charging between soda and salt. Otherwise, the ambient detrimental forces may be absorbed along with the arealoha forces. My findings do not agree with this. None of my subjects ever noticed detrimental effects from having the fingers pointing north while working with salt and soda.

Nixon's next recommendation was not to hold the hand too far down between the compounds. My subjects felt the magnetic pull and the mushy field low between the compounds. She also said to avoid absorbing the forces during the three days around the new and the full moon. The theory is that solar and lunar energy is stronger at this time, and someone already under stress might get even more stressed out. But my experience is that these are amplification times, rather than detrimental ones. I found that if you can keep your own energies flowing, the new and full moon periods will enhance whatever you are doing. Another recommendation of Nixon's was to avoid using more than two jars of compounds at any one time and in any combination other than east and west. My experimentation with this is too limited for me to comment on it further. Finally, she said not to absorb the arealoha energies in one hand only. This has not proven detrimental in any of the tests I have carried out, but the effects are greater when two hands are used.

After all the avoidances have been observed and the jars are properly set up, the procedure is simple: 1) lower the head away from the jars for eight seconds to bring a supply of blood to all the head receptors; 2) lift the head and hold the right hand above and between the jars for six seconds, repeating with the left hand; 3) dip each finger of the right hand plus the thumb into the energy stream and repeat with the left hand, being careful to give equal time to each; 4) jog around the room for about sixty seconds to bring the forces to the feet receptors; 5) neutralize by the accordion method and deep breathing for six cycles.

This is an interesting ritual, but in my experience mostly unnecessary. With the salt west, just putting the fingers in bowls of the dissolved compounds, or placing one hand on each compound, gives a very good and lasting charge.

## Vivaxis Induction

Another significant discovery of Frances Nixon parallels some of my own research on inducted fields. This experimentation starts with the recognition that a lightning strike can create a powerful vivaxis. Nixon located one centered on a fir tree that was known to have retained its strength for fifteen years and possibly much longer. The fir tree was still alive and showed signs of trying to heal over the twenty-five foot scar. With her dowsing instruments, Nixon recorded a vivaxis with a twenty-five-foot radius extending out from the tree on all sides, with an inner core seven feet in diameter, centered at the base of the tree. Nixon suggested that it would be devastating to have such an energy field centered in one's home because of the effect it would have on a person's own circuit and nervous system. This follows her thesis that exposure to vivaxes other than one's own should be as brief as possible, and adequate steps should be taken to erase their effects without delay.

I disagree with this to a certain extent. For one thing, the Native Americans in certain areas practiced standing with their backs to large trees with arms spread, in order to absorb some of the tree's energy. Also, they recognized certain sacred spots which were energy centers where energies could be replenished and a super amount of power gained. Such power spots are commonly acknowledged in the traditions of peoples all over the world. It is known that some people can absorb the energy freely in a strong field of *vril* and gain strength from it, while others may grow dizzy and faint and suffer nausea and body aches. In one of Reich's experiments with radium and orgone, such an intense vivaxis was created that no one except Reich himself could enter the field without getting ill.

I believe that one's reaction depends on blocks or freedom from blocks in the personal energy circuit. If there are many blocks the incoming energy cannot flow freely and causes adverse reactions. With few or no blocks a person can beneficially absorb practically all the *vril* that can be put into his or her system. In a similar vein, I believe that the temporary effects of vivaxis channeling are not so much due to the interference from foreign energy fields as to the reblocking of the personal circuit because of subconscious complexes. Reich found that orgone treatments had to be supplemented by mental therapy to be permanently effective. I think the same is true of vivaxis channeling.

To return to the tree, Nixon created an artificial vivaxis near her home for a calcium tablet. She brought it into the center core of the lightning vivaxis. Then three-and-a-half miles from the tree she put a leaf on the tablet's vivaxis. The original vivaxis of the tablet was only the size of the tablet, but in the lightning core it instantly assumed the size and strength of the field into which it had been placed, which was seven feet in diameter. The energy of the stronger field had been inducted over a distance of three-and-a-half miles! This is similar to the effect produced with a signature and a Manabox, and to a later experiment with a signature in the force field between sea salt and soda. There is also a correlation between the use of witnesses or links in radionics and psychotronics.

When the tablet was removed from the lightning field, of course the duplicate field disappeared. But after only five minutes the leaf's field became linked to the core field and retained a seven-foot field itself, even after the calcium tablet was destroyed. And over a period of years, kept from direct sunlight, this leaf stayed green and flexible, while a leaf from the same tree picked at the same time became dry and brittle. Such leaves, said Nixon, *have a mummified appearance* like the *vril* effect of a pyramid or similar device. It would be interesting to find out whether other *vril* effects, such as the mummification of meat, the alteration of liquids and the sharpening of razor blades could also be obtained by induction.

Frances Nixon made some very important discoveries about *vril*. Hopefully her work will stimulate research that will produce even more useful techniques and ideas.

### On Absorbing Energy

Nixon wrote a lot about absorbing energies, and I have gone along with the concept to simplify the presentation. But I would like to end this chapter with some comments on that concept.

Many people think of energy as a fluid like water, which can fill a container or be soaked up by a sponge, make you clean or dirty, be pumped into you or drained away, make you healthy and strong or poison and weaken you. With such an analogy, it makes sense to talk about absorbing it, neutralizing it, protecting yourself from drainage, and being concerned about contamination.

However, this liquid concept of energy, though useful sometimes, is a poor analogy, not only because it is limiting, but because it is very different from what we actually know about energy. Much more useful and closer to experience is the wave or vibration analogy. A wave moves through water but is not the water itself. Energy is really movement, and the characteristics of movement are speed (frequency or rate of vibration: the number of waves in a given distance or time period); strength (amplitude: the height of a wave); shape (form or pattern); and size (field, or area of influence). Power, then, is the ability to influence movement/energy—its speed, strength, shape or size and resonance—by causing it to vibrate in synch with an external source of stimulation. Resistance occurs when one field tries to influence another field too different from itself, like waves crashing against rock.

In this view, we are constantly moving in and out of energy fields, influencing some and being influenced by others. Strong fields can influence us in a strong way, to the degree that we are in resonance with them. But to the degree that we are not in resonance, we will resist that influence or change of movement. If the external field is strong enough and our resistance is intense enough, we could experience unpleasant effects. So some people experience pleasure in a pyramid, an orgone box or a powerful vivaxis, and others experience pain. This is not because the external field is good or bad but because it either matches one's own field or not.

Fortunately, human beings can change both their internal and external environments for harmonious and healing purposes, and that is the subject of the next chapter.

# 9
# Geomancy: Harmonizing Yin and Yang

The oldest energy technology of all—far older than the pyramids or Egypt or the most ancient tales of flying and destruction from India and China—is also the simplest. This technology combines a deep awareness of the energy patterns of nature with the creative imagination of the human mind. The most familiar English term for this technology is both misleading and inadequate, but it is growing in use. Since nothing better has turned up, I will use it—"geomancy." Unfortunately, that term implies only a passive awareness, but this technology also has an active side. We could call it "geomantic engineering," though I prefer "geomagic." However, I will stick with "geomancy" as a generic term.

The essentials of this technology are based on several important assumptions: 1) the visible, tangible world is generated by an invisible and dynamic matrix of energy; 2) this energy has two polarities which are not absolute, but which are relative and transformative and can change into each other; 3) these polarities have an influential field effect which may be harmonious or inharmonious; and 4) either mental or physical action can change the effects of the polarities or the polarities themselves.

**176**

## Feng Shui

The term *Feng Shui,* by which Chinese geomancy is known, means "wind water." It refers not so much to the natural elements themselves as to the forces they symbolize—the two polarities of *vril* which are also called *yang* and *yin.* Relatively speaking, *yang* expresses itself as hardness, whiteness, brightness, highness, straightness, maleness, stimulation and activity; while *yin* expresses itself as softness, blackness, dimness, lowness, curviness, femaleness, sedation and receptivity. An excess of *yang* in the body produces tension, swelling and infection; in the emotions it produces anger, jealousy and resentment; and in the environment hyperactivity, violence and destruction. An excess of *yin* in the body produces flabbiness, weakness and lethargy; in the emotions fear, anxiety and guilt; and in the environment apathy, solitude and stagnation. The purpose of *Feng Shui* is to establish a harmonious balance between *yang* and *yin,* either by changing attitude, changing location or changing the physical environment itself. The purpose of the harmonious balance is to enhance the three most important factors that concern the ordinary Chinese: health, wealth and sex. Harmonious balance, however, does not mean equality. The ideal harmony is about 60 percent *yang* to 40 percent *yin,* roughly the ideal balance between positive and negative ions in the air.

Acupuncture is actually a highly specialized branch of *Feng Shui* which uses the hands, the eyes, needles, herbs and sometimes electricity to diagnose and correct the geomancy of the body. The modern practice called *Feng Shui,* however, is primarily concerned with architecture and landscaping and their relation to the natural environment, including society. The practitioners of *Feng Shui* use observation, intuition and imagination as tools in their work. More traditional practitioners may also use a kind of circular chart, often engraved on metal, called a *lo pan*. Although most of their work is still done in Hong Kong, Taiwan and Japan, *Feng Shui* practitioners are often called upon by people in other countries to increase business or harmony.

As a science, *Feng Shui* is concerned with the lay of the land, that is, the relationship between mountains, hills, rivers, valleys and compass directions; the placement, design, materials and colors of buildings and rooms within those buildings; and the relationship with surrounding buildings and other humanly made structures such as roads and powerlines. As an art, *Feng Shui* also deals with symbols, omens and their interpretation. Some *Feng Shui* practitioners lean toward the scientific side and some toward the artistic.

There is a story that a bank in Hong Kong was doing poorly, so they called in a *Feng Shui* expert to help. He examined the building inside and out and made recommendations for extensive remodeling to correct the imbalance of energies. Because those recommendations were too expensive, the bank directors called in another *Feng Shui* practitioner for a second opinion. This one also examined the bank inside and out and then announced that the problem was a nearby hill which resembled a crouching lion about to attack the bank. This excessive *yang* energy directed toward the bank was keeping the customers away. He recommended simply covering the front of the bank with mirrors to reflect the lion's energy away. Since this was not expensive, the bankers followed the recommendation. Their business immediately increased. Since *Feng Shui* is a world where energy and expectation work hand in hand, there is no way to analyze this story in Western terms. The important thing is that it worked.

## Hawaiian Geomancy

In old Hawaii geomancy and its practitioners were called by an odd name, *kuhikuhipu'uone,* which means "to point out the sane dunes." The outer meaning of this name came from their training exercises in which they practiced locating objects hidden in the sand in order to attune themselves to subtle energies. The hidden meaning is in the word *kuhi,* whose roots *ku* and *hi* represent the same concepts as *yang* and *yin,* respectively.

Hawaiian geomancers were seers, psychics and magicians, as well as architects. They planned and laid out temples, homes, fish ponds and social activities and located fresh water. In addition to observation, intuition and imagination, their tools included a type of dowsing rod called a *paoa,* a dowsing staff called *'au,* and a measuring cord, *aha.*

*Feng Shui* and the Hawaiian version have their origin in myths. Legends of Pele, the volcano goddess, tell of her coming to the Hawaiian Islands and dowsing caves and pits until she found the earthly fire where she could make her home. Other legends tell of the gods Kane and Kanaloa who struck rocks with their magical staves, whereupon fresh water springs flowed out. It is said that the homes of some early missionaries who did not listen to the geomancers were blown away by strong winds or shaken to pieces by earthquakes.

## Basic Concepts

I use the specific and well-known terms *yang* and *yin* to denote the polarities of *vril.* The characteristics of *yang/yin* are not absolute but relative to each other. A ruby crystal is harder than a quartz crystal, for example, but a ruby is softer than a diamond. Likewise,

a man is *yang* and a woman is *yin,* but a female
Amazon warrior is more *yang* than a Zen monk.

## Power Spots

A power spot is any location with a higher energy
intensity than its surroundings. Power spots are relative
and exist only in relationship to the surroundings.
Their *yang* or *yin* nature also depends on what they are
being compared to. As an example, Los Angeles can be
considered very *yang* in relation to Honolulu, which is
*yin* by comparison. On the other hand, Honolulu is
*yang* when compared to Kauai, a comparatively *yin*
island. Still, certain features of the land and of architecture have characteristic polarities.

*Yang* spots: Heights, peaks and summits are *yang.*
This includes hilltops, mountaintops, ridgelines and
rooftops. Angular areas and angular enclosures are also
*yang* spots. A square building is *yang* compared to the
outside, and within the building the high *yang* spots
are the corners. The most *yang* corners are those on
the highest floors, as long as nothing modifies them.
The center of any triangle formed by three objects,
such as boulders or trees is a *yang* spot. Dry areas,
rocky areas, and open areas like meadows (compared to
the woods) and bare courtyards (compared to interiors)
are other *yang* spots. Population centers or group
activity centers are *yang;* the more people the higher
the *yang* energy. Places where machinery operates,
areas near or under transformers and electrical power
lines, and areas near or on busy highways or freeways
are *yang,* as are currently empty places that have been
locations of intense activity, like lightning-struck
objects, stadiums, battlefields and playgrounds. The
latter relate to the vivaxis idea. Any of the above are
places you could go to increase your *yang* energy.

*Yin* spots: Valleys, canyons, ravines, glens, caves and holes are all *yin*. Caves also have the highest natural concentration of negative ions that tend to induce calmness and relaxation. Curved areas, like bays and even bay windows, and curved enclosures are *yin*. A bare courtyard might be *yang* compared to an interior, but a round courtyard is more *yin* than a square one. A circle of trees or boulders is *yin*. Wet areas, like oases, shorelines, marshes and swamps, and places next to waterfalls, fountains and moving water are good *yin* spots. So are any places where plants grow, whether rain forests, jungles, woods, forests, gardens, orchards, fields or the plant section of a department store. Areas of low population and little activity are *yin*. A hermit living on a mountaintop is in a *yin* spot compared to a city, but a hermit living in a cave at the base of the mountain is in an even stronger *yin* spot. Structures like churches, meditation centers and medicine wheels are *yin,* too.

## Power (Ley) Lines

There are two kinds of power lines in geomancy—those that conduct *vril* along visible channels and those that conduct it along invisible channels.

Visible channels in the natural world are either curved (*yin*), like stream and river beds, or straight (*yang*), like fault lines. Natural invisible lines follow both the relatively straight electromagnetic lines of force and a mysterious set of curved lines of force. Hawaiian tradition contains tantalizing clues of this second pathway in chants about thoughts that *undulate* toward their destination. Other clues are suggested by wind and ocean currents that curve without relation to physical land masses.

Visible *vril* lines made by humans are created by

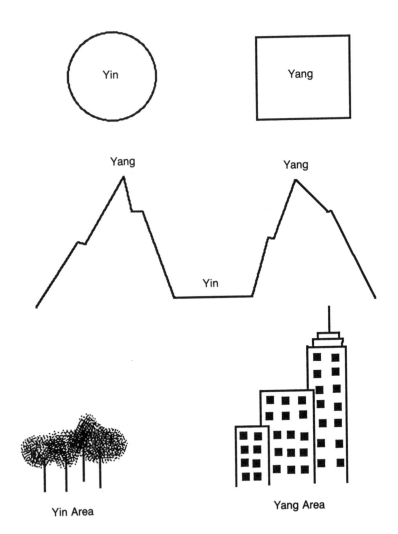

Yin

Yang

Yang

Yang

Yin

Yin Area

Yang Area

paths, roads, highways, train tracks and electrical power lines. A road map of any country is also a good map of ley lines and power spots, and invisible *vril* lines are created by regular air and sea routes. Another kind of invisible line is created by mentally linking any two power spots. Some people today do that when they make maps of invisible "power grids" that supposedly cover the earth. These are generally straight line grids that link power spots the mapmaker thinks are significant (not all such maps agree on this). Sometimes the straight line bias indicates areas as power spots that have no history of being significant. These grid maps may be valid, but they should be treated as mental constructs and not necessarily natural.

To use a *vril* line, stand on it or be in it and attempt to feel the energy flow. For highways, train tracks, sea and air routes, it is easier and safer to sit in an appropriate vehicle. The "gridlines" produce a good effect when you link two power spots in your mind and face one or the other, somewhat like "channeling" a vivaxis.

### Power Times

Power times in geomancy relate to recurring and special events, natural energy increases and symbolic ones.

One of the oldest recognized power times is sunrise, when there is a definite change in the energy field of the area being lit. If you have any sensitivity at all, you can actually feel the change of energy and the quickening of activity, above and beyond the sights and sounds. This is the changeover from the *yin* of night to the *yang* of day. Noon is the height of *yang* intensity for most places in the world, though in the extreme north and south it is more symbolic. In old Hawaii, teaching was given between sunrise and noon, to take advantage of the increasing *yang* energy. Sunset, naturally, is another power time, when the *yin* energy of night begins to increase, reaching its peak at midnight. In old Hawaii, sunset was considered the beginning of the new "day" because creativity takes place in the unseen world of mind or spirit, symbolized by nighttime, and manifestation occurs in the outer, visible world, symbolized by daytime. Most people can feel the peaceful relaxation that pervades the world at sunset, and some cultures like the Japanese honor it with ritual.

The cycles of the moon also play an important part in geomancy. Since everything is relative, the times of new and full moon are both *yang,* and the times of quarter moons (actually half moons) are both *yin.* Historically, a favored time for planting and initiating projects is between the new and full moons when *yang* energy is supposed to be on the increase, but this is mostly symbolic. In terms of actual energy effects, new moon is a *yang* energy peak. The *yang* diminishes to *yin* until first quarter, then increases until full, decreases to third quarter, and increases again to new. Some cultures recognized this by planting only during the three days around the new and full moons. In Hawaii these were times for external activity, and the quarter moon periods were times for rest, mending and prayer.

Periods of seasonal change are power times, but specific dates and moments are more symbolic than natural. March 21 at 3:10 P.M. is the exact moment when the sun is equidistant between its highest and lowest positions and the lengths of day and night are roughly equal (depending on the latitude). But in terms of nature's energy moving from the *yin* of winter to the *yang* of spring, the first leaf, the first flower, the first lamb or, in the tropics, the first appearance of flying fish are all more significant. We Westerners tend to worship exactness, but nature is not always so exact. Nevertheless, the symbolic points of change created by different cultures are still times of great power, and they influence human thought and feelings in particular ways.

Easter, named after an ancient Germanic goddess, in modern times is calculated as the first Sunday after the first full moon after the vernal equinox. It is a powerful *yang* time. So is May Day, which does not correspond to any natural event except that it happens to be roughly midway between the spring equinox and the summer solstice. The latter is called midsummer by the English and the beginning of summer by the Americans. Modern social practice tends to ignore the fall equinox, but some areas celebrate the first full moon after it as a harvest moon. Hallowe'en, an ancient celebration of the midpoint between the fall equinox and the winter solstice, is still a powerful *yin* time, and Christmas or Yule, falling three days after the winter solstice, would be except for the shopping frenzy. January 1, an arbitrary date, is a powerful *yang* time because it symbolizes the beginning of a new life for so many people.

In terms of natural and more or less irregular events, the periods of high and low energy systems are both *yang* times. In high pressure systems *yang* energy is characterized by clear skies, dry and still air; in low pressure systems the winds preceding a storm carry a strong charge of positive ions, *yang* energy, which increases physical and emotional stress for some. People with arthritis and rheumatism often actually feel an approaching storm in their bones. When the rain finally falls, a time of *yin* energy begins. It corresponds to the creation of abundant negative ions from the falling water. Another high *yang* time occurs when dry winds generate a very high count of positive ions through friction with the surfaces they travel over. These are the "crazy-making" winds of the Harmattan in West Africa, the Scirocco in the Mediterranean, the Santa Anas in California and the Kona winds in Hawaii.

Taking advantage of power times requires awareness, attention and imagination. First, be aware of whether it is a *yang* or *yin* time; then put your attention on the effects you want from it. Finally, use your imagination to maintain a positive focus and a positive expectation.

## Power Colors

Colors do not just have energy; they *are* energy. When we see a color, we are struck by reflections of light energy. And not just in our eyes. The reflected energy can affect our personal *vril* field as well as our physical body, for color, in addition to its light energy, has *vril* effects, too. A simple example is "sun tea." When tea bags are placed in a clear glass jar of water and left in the sun for a while, they produce a smooth and mellow tea that tastes like tea placed in a pyramid or on a Manabox. Also, water "charged" or left in the sun in a green bottle induces house plants to develop a strong root system and very green leaves. It is good to drink, too, tasting like water charged in a *vril* device.

In general, the warm colors—red, orange and yellow—radiate *yang* energy, and the cool colors—green, blue and violet—radiate *yin*. Because of relativity, however, an electric blue would be more *yang* than a dusty pink. The brighter the color the more *yang*, and the duller it is the more *yin*. Comparatively, white is *yang* and black and gray are *yin*, though a solid black can "out*yang*" any dull color. Consider the intimidating force of the black robes of a priest or the black of formal dress.

When either black or white are next to another color, they have the effect of making that color more *yang*. Think of a green tablecloth compared to a green and white checked one or a red blanket compared to a red and black plaid one. When either white or black is blended with other colors, however, it makes the colors more *yin*. Think of the difference between a royal blue jacket and a sky blue one, or between orange shoes and brown ones.

The easiest way to use the *vril* energies of colors is in your wardrobe or your environment. When you pick colors for clothing, consider the effect on others as well as on yourself. In your environment, think of how you want to use the space, remembering that *yang* stimulates and *yin* calms. Another good idea is to have objects of specific colors to meditate with for particular effects. A friend gave me a card about 5″ x 7″ with a geometric design that was red on one side and blue on the other. Just gazing at the red side stimulates my energy and gazing at the blue side calms me down.

### Territorial Energy

As human animals we not only have a strong herd or pack instinct (though we have our share of lone wolves, rogue elephants and hermit dolphins), but we are highly territorial. Like many other animals, our sense of territory extends both physically and socially. That is, we establish invisible borders around our bodies, our property and our possessions; and also around our social groupings of family, friends, neighborhoods, clubs, community, nation, hemisphere, etc. Our instinctive tendency, stronger in some than others, is to care for our territory and protect it from invasion or appropriation. Sometimes, in order to make our own territory seem better, we might diminish the value or importance of other territories; or, in order to make ourselves seem better, we might invade or appropriate the territory of others. Generally speaking, the more insecure we feel, the stronger is our tendency to protect or increase our territory. And the more secure we feel, the stronger is our tendency to open our borders or even change them. Unlike other animals, we extend our sense of territory into mental and psychic realms. We have copyright laws for the products of our imagination; rivalry between different philosophies, theories and religions; techniques for shielding our auras from the telepathy of others; and reservations about (if not fear of) being visited in our dreams.

The essential nature of a territory is that it is unique and different from other territories. In ancient times this difference was personified as the spirit of the territory, which today we might call its energy pattern. Thus, ancient peoples all over the world gave special names to the spirits, or patterns, of people, places, things and events. Since each territory and spirit/pattern was distinctive, the borders between territories were considered tremendously important because they were patternless or unstable areas where anything might happen. They could be sacred spaces or moments which could bring blessings, or else non-places—like a no-man's land—where chaos reigned. The ancients' main way of dealing with this was to establish rituals—special patterns of prayer and/or action—for crossing from one territory to another. This practice gave rise to annual and seasonal celebrations, moon phase rituals, sunrise and sunset rituals, and rituals for every kind of beginning or ending, entering or leaving, transition or change. Thus the threshold of a house, a crossroads, a river, the entrance to a cave and a gate were all treated as sacred places. In ancient Hawaii, as an example, elaborate rituals were conducted every year both to mark the year and to rededicate the borders of all the districts on each island. Among the Maori people of New Zealand, the meeting house is considered a living spirit. In its courtyard, *marae,* elaborate territorial rituals are still conducted whenever a visiting group from another territory is received, in order to harmonize the different spirits or energies.

Since territoriality and energy awareness are instinctive, which experience leads us to believe, then we might benefit by paying much more attention to the energies at the borders of our own bodies, minds, spirit and environment. I believe that the whole concept and experience of territoriality is linked to an instinctive awareness of real energy patterns, and especially to the borders between patterns. If we think of everything in terms of energy, and of all energy in terms of *yang* and *yin,* then the borders between all things, whether physical or not, are neither *yang* nor *yin.* The *vril* there is open, without pattern, chaotic. In that area anything could happen. You may have either experienced or seen movies of someone walking across a border into a neutral zone between two sentry posts. You feel the tension and the agony of wondering whether the person will be stopped and called back or allowed to continue toward safety. In the country behind, danger is definite; in the country ahead, safety is definite. But in between everything is in potential.

Because the energy at borders is patternless, they are ideal places in which to use the power of your mind to influence *vril.* You can call the process prayer, programming, creative meditation or whatever. Sometimes the difficulty in turning our dreams into reality is that the patterns we are trying to bring into being are too different from the prevailing patterns around us. One solution is to move to a more suitable environment, but another is to make our plans and focus our thoughts in a border area.

As a general guide, borders include entrances, exits, edges and thresholds—not only those leading into or out of buildings, but also those between rooms and between any two distinct areas, such as different floor levels in a big room—stairways and stairwells, the line between a meadow and woods, the entrance to a cave, the bank of a river or a beach, or the edge of a cliff; and also the moments of waking or falling asleep.

Borders also include meeting points where very different energies commingle, such as the periods of dawn and twilight; places of prayer and meditation, like churches and chapels, sacred groves and temples (border areas between the outer and inner worlds); and places designated by human beings as neutral zones.

### Geomantic Healing

There are complicated systems for using geomancy to heal or harmonize, but the basic process is simple: when in doubt, change something to its relative opposite. Soften what is too hard and harden what is too soft; lower what is too high and lift what is too low; shorten what is too long and lengthen what is too short; activate what is too inactive and deactivate what is too active; straighten what is too curved and curve what is too straight. In the following sections are examples for different kinds of geomantic healing.

### Personal Geomancy

When things are not working well in your life, whether physically, emotionally, financially, etc., you need to change something that you are doing. In terms of geomancy, first identify any behavior that carries an excess of *yang* or *yin* energy. Then do something that is its relative opposite. For instance, you might check your voice pattern. If it is high, fast and strained, practice making it low, slow and relaxed, or vice versa. Check your breathing pattern, too. Most often under stress breathing is shallow and needs to be deepened. Posture is also important from a geomantic point of view. A straight and rigid posture is good for analytical learning and thinking and tends to induce feelings of strength and confidence. But when overdone it tends to separate you emotionally from others and inhibit your flexibility. A softer, more relaxed posture tends to invite compassion and friendship and is good for intuitive learning and thinking. But if overdone it tends to induce apathy, depression and a lack of sympathy or help from others. Other things to check and possibly change are work/rest cycles, outer/inner activity cycles and even dietary habits.

Whatever your personal problem, changing any pattern tends to loosen up your whole energy system and facilitate a solution. If I change my diet, for instance, it is not to improve health but to change patterns, although better health usually results no matter what the diet change is. One of the most useful personal pattern changes I have found, besides deeper breathing, is to take frequent, short breaks from my work routine every day, no matter what the routine for that day is. On a day of study and quiet research, about once an hour I take activity breaks of work or exercise of thirty seconds to five minutes. On a day of dynamic activity, I take frequent rest breaks for reading or meditation.

## Social Geomancy

In working with social energy patterns, you need to be aware of group reactions and relationships, the social ambiance, the relative positions of the people, the presence or lack of organization, ongoing activities and the purpose or goals of the group. Again, to coin words, you want to *yangify* what is too *yin,* and *yinify* what is too *yang.*

You may have heard that in some companies the choice office is in a corner. This is true for reasons of geomancy as well as psychology, because corners have high *yang* energy. Business leaders tend to work on or near the top floor of an office building, and community leaders tend to live on or near the top of a hill, both of which are *yang* spots. On the other hand, revolutionary leaders tend to come from *yin* areas like the slums rather than the rich, neat areas or the countryside rather than the city whenever these areas become extreme in their *yangness* or their *yinness.*

Group meetings are usually arranged in a *yang* manner, with chairs and tables in straight rows and columns, or in a *yin* manner, with chairs set in a circle, a half circle or just scattered. *Yang* arrangements are good for analytical discussion, lectures with factual information, scientific or technological learning and formal meetings where rules and procedures are important. *Yin* arrangements are good for creative work, learning skills and socializing.

### Environmental Geomancy

Energy patterns in the environment are found in landscaping, placement and structure of buildings, natural and artificial vivaxes, and the placement of power objects and patterns.

In my opinion, the greatest landscape artists have come from the Chinese, Japanese, Celtic and English cultures. The first three tend toward producing *yin* effects, and the latter is usually quite *yang.* Good landscaping can set up strong *vril* fields that have a powerful influence on the people moving through them. At its most basic, *yang* landscaping involves neat rows and straight paths, while *yin* landscaping involves lots of meanders and curves.

Without calling in a *Feng Shui* expert or a geomantically oriented architect or interior designer, you can do simple things for the exterior and interior of your home or office to increase the harmony of the energies. Follow the simple principle of moving any excess toward its relative opposite. On my own home, for instance, I had a contractor add shingles to the peaks and corners of my roof, so that all the straight ridge lines curved up slightly at the ends. It evokes a Japanese flavor, but I did it because I have found that very straight roof lines tend to increase tension in a house, while slight curves on the ends helps make life inside and outside more harmonious. Trees and shrubs also soften the *yang* energy of excessive straight lines in a building.

A special aspect of environmental geomancy is the labyrinth. This is a maze that runs in a continuous line without any dead ends or traps. Its purpose is not to trick, but to focus mind and energy for a defined purpose. In many places of the world labyrinths were (and are) used for group ceremonies, but some are also used for individual meditation, energizing, manifesting or spiritual questing. While in Denmark, I visited a replica of a Stone Age village. On a hilltop was a reproduction of a Celtic labyrinth that ancient Swedes used to dance along in seasonal celebrations. As I walked the curved labyrinth, I could feel myself being charged with a deeply calming energy. It is interesting that the pattern of the Celtic labyrinth is virtually identical to the *Tápu'at*, Mother Earth symbol of the Hopi (see below), and to the Labyrinth of Daedelus which was used for the Minotaur in ancient Crete. Also interesting is the fact that the Hopi symbol has a *yang* and a *yin* version.

Celtic Labyrinth        Hopi *yin* version        Hopi *yang* version

In Western society interiors are commonly too *yang,* which can aggravate physical, emotional and mental stress. The easiest way to soften an excessively *yang* room is to put plants in it. Spider plants and ferns are an excellent choice because they give off negative ions, but any plants will help. Anything curved, like lamps and lampshades, round tables, curved lines on furniture, art or sculpture with rounded lines and flowing draperies adds to the *yin* effect. Straight beams, cornices and furniture, straight or square patterns on the walls, squared windows and doors, venetian blinds and straight or squared floor patterns all increase the *yang* energy. I was once asked to help a young boy who was having nightmares, and my intuition led me to ask to see his room. It could hardly have been more *yang*—basically white, bare and square. Even his bed, dresser and single chair were all angular. I recommended plants, paintings or photos of nature, rounded objects and painting curved patterns on the walls. Some of these things were done, and the last I heard he was sleeping much better.

My favorite story concerns a couple who had taken one of my courses that includes geomancy. They found themselves staying for a few days in a stark and straight hotel room. The woman was unable to sleep and was becoming nervous and jittery. Applying the principle of relative opposites, the man came up with a marvelous emergency solution. Every night, before going to bed, he draped the whole room with great loops of toilet tissue, and every morning he took them down so as not to startle the maid. His wife slept wonderfully for the rest of their stay.

### Symbolic Geomancy

For untold ages human beings have used symbolic objects and rituals to increase, accumulate and influence the actions of *vril*. Amulets and talismans are known and used all over the world. Even in the West where they are "officially" disdained, people use and benefit from such things as lucky charms, religious medals and crystals. Apart from an object's natural energy, specific powers attributed to it that are not extensions of its physical characteristics are often based on belief and expectation. But rather than turning away from such objects, you can use them with that in mind.

An amethyst crystal cuts glass. It was also used by the ancient Greeks to cure drunkenness (because it is the color of wine) and is used today by crystal healers to raise consciousness and to inspire (because purple is considered a high vibration). The first quality is a natural extension of the crystal's physical characteristics, but the next two are based on belief and expectation. These two uses turn the crystal into an amulet. And the wonderful thing is that if you allow yourself to believe, you get the effects.

Amulets and talismans designated as having special powers are empowered by the user. Any effects come about because the user believes it will, at least at some level of consciousness. Because of that, you can turn any object you choose into an amulet or talisman. When you designate an object as having special

powers, say of healing or attracting wealth, you are
actually using that object to stimulate those powers
within yourself. The more natural *vril* the object has
and the more it stirs up resonant emotional energies
within you, the more effective it is. Crystals, because of
their natural energy and beauty, make good amulets, as
do shells and many religious and cultural symbols. You
can either go along with the power said to be in an
object, or you can invest it with any power you choose.
I am an inveterate collector, and I have all kinds of
objects around my home. Instead of just looking at
them, I give them all powers, and I remind them of
their powers every time I see or touch them. I have
objects for increasing happiness, harmony and love; for
attracting money; for giving me confidence; and for
whatever I need at the moment. I know this is only a
way of giving myself subliminal suggestions, but it
works, and my personal *vril* field interacts with the
environment to manifest what I want.

I have discussed the nature and structure of ritual in
my book *Urban Shaman.* Here I share a few simple
geomantic rituals for influencing personal, social and
environmental *vril.*

The ritual I call "flow patterns" resembles Pavlita's
stare patterns. The first flow pattern is based on
ancient energy ideas found all over the world, that the
polarities of *vril* flow in opposite directions to each
other and have opposite effects. I call the polarities by
the old European terms *deosil* and *widdershins. Deosil*
is a clockwise movement, either circular or spiral, and
*widdershins* is a counterwise movement. When used
symbolically, *deosil* has the *yang* effects of manifestation, connecting and movement outward into the
physical world, while *widdershins* has the *yin* effects
of undoing, disconnecting, and movement inward to
the world of spirit. Or even simpler, *deosil* stimulates

and *widdershins* calms. The specific effects depend on your focus. In ancient times people would dance *deosil* in the spring to fertilize the crops and the women, and dance *widdershins* in the fall to pull the energies of life back into the safety of earth's bosom.

You can use this symbolic practice: Make a circle. In the center put an object that represents what you want or a photo of someone you want to help. Use your finger, a pencil, a rod or a crystal to revolve the object in a direction corresponding to your intent, while keeping that intent strongly in mind. This becomes a simple type of psychotronic device.

The second type of flow pattern utilizes the infinity symbol. First, put two symbolic objects near each other. Move your finger, pencil, rod or crystal in a figure eight pattern around both objects while focusing on a harmonious relationship between what the objects represent. For both of the flow patterns, continue focusing until you feel like stopping.

The use of "spirit" patterns brings us back to one of the original meanings of geomancy, "divination by means of the earth." To teach this I have students find twenty-five natural objects of not more than an inch in length or diameter, all roughly the same size, usually sticks, stones and maybe shells. The objects can be of different kinds or all the same. You may want to make a special set for yourself. One of my favorites consists of cowrie shells.

In the process, first focus on some issue of interest or concern, and then toss the objects out in front of you as you would throw dice. Then sit with the resulting pattern and try to feel it as a pattern of energy. You can try to interpret it intellectually if you want, but it is not necessary. After you have gotten the feel of it, carefully adjust or move any of the pieces until the whole feels "right." You might move a few objects, sit with the new pattern, move some more, sit with that, and so on until you are comfortable with the configuration. Then sit with that until you feel like doing something else.

The idea is that the first toss of the objects produces an external pattern that reflects the inner one. When you first focus you are tuning into a part of your *vril* field which matches the pattern of the situation you are focusing on. Sitting with that increases your subconscious knowledge of the stresses and strains in the pattern that are inhibiting a harmonious resolution. When you follow your instinct and intuition to change the pattern, you are guided by that subconscious knowledge. And sitting with the comfortable external pattern creates a resonance within you that begins to move the larger *vril* field in ways that bring about a manifested resolution.

Tuning into and using the natural energies of the Earth can assist you in your health and well-being. In addition, the very act of applying geomancy will tend to expand your awareness and stimulate your spiritual growth. After a short period of such practice you will find that the perception of energetic relationships in your environment will become almost habitual, and your appreciation of the one life that pervades everything will increase greatly.

# 10
# Extra Energy

It is not possible to put into one short chapter all that remains to be said about the various sources and discoveries concerning *vril*. Therefore I am being arbitrary in presenting what is to come. What I have chosen is important, but that does not imply that what is not included is not. The final test, as I see it, is applicability; yet few discoveries are immediately applicable. Caution and patience are needed in evaluating the worth of all these discoveries.

## Cameron's Cones

Cones and coils were mentioned briefly in previous chapters, and here they are discussed in greater detail. Verne Cameron, a professional dowser, is credited with being the real pioneer in this area. While trying to improve his dowsing results, he stumbled on a mysterious emanation from cones and coils. He was toying with using a coil to collect and strengthen the radiations supposedly rising from underground water flows. That did not work, but in the process Cameron discovered that the coils and cones themselves seemed to emit a kind of radiation. Flat coils placed horizontally emitted a force both upward and downward. There is some question as to whether an effect emitted in one direction is more detrimental than in another. But the quality of the energy changes when the coils are flipped over, so the change depends on the direction of the winding, clockwise or counterclockwise, rather than the direction of the flow.

The first coils used by Cameron were metallic strips ½" to 1" wide, insulated, and wound onto themselves to form a flat disk. He found that a flat helix of insulated wires gave the same results. Diameter did not seem to make any difference. For the most part he worked with coils of eight to twelve or more inches long. I do not know why he specified insulated wire, unless he still thought he was dealing with a form of electromagnetism (he became convinced later that it was not electrical, at least). I have found that bare wire works about as well for getting *vril* effects, but if there is any difference it may be due to a Reichian effect between the metal and the insulator. Of course, the wires were not connected to any power source.

The cones used by Cameron were made of zinc, sheet iron or aluminum for the most part, but cardboard worked if lined inside and out with aluminum foil (the Reichian/capacitor effect). There are conflicting stories about how Cameron first noticed the "cone rays," as he called them, but probably it was an outgrowth of his coil experiments. He found that increasing the number of coils or turns of wire consecutively in the same place made no difference in their energy output. At first this led him to use flat spirals of wire, but then he was able to obtain more energy output with a helix (a three-dimensional spiral).

While outlining the shape of the energy field of the helix with his dowser, Cameron noticed that it formed a 90-degree invisible cone. So he wondered what would happen if he used an actual cone. When he made one out of tin, two feet in diameter with a 90-degree angle at the top, it projected a beam of energy from its tip as powerful as was emitted by a group of five coils he had previously made. This beam was about an inch in diameter and extended to an unknown distance with undiminished force. If the angle were less than 90 degrees the beam was shortened and brought to a focus, but if greater than 90 degrees it tended to disperse. I have found the same effect in working with domes, which could be described as rounded off cones.

Cameron carried out a number of objective experiments to prove that the energy he was recording was real. After learning that the energy could be carried along a wire, he connected three cones in series, then laid the lead wire under a plot of ground a few inches below the surface. A package of radish seeds was divided, with one half planted over the wire and the other half (the controls) planted ten feet away. Both received the same amount of water and suffered the same climatic conditions. The controls grew normally, but the test plants hardly grew at all. This corresponds exactly with my own plant experiments in which an excess of *vril* either inhibits growth or kills young plants. Enough of an excess even kills trees, as Reich found out.

Another test of Cameron's demonstrated the relationship between his cone energy and other *vril* sources. Using the same three cones in series, he held the point of the lead wire against a long-standing trichina infection on his arm for twenty minutes. According to his report, it killed the infection and did not affect the healthy tissues.

Cameron generally laid pyramids on a flat surface and oriented them to the north. Cones work best, according to Cameron, when hung from the edge and placed six feet or more above the ground. "Working best" seems to mean that they emit more energy when so placed. Cameron believed that the energy was collected or accumulated from the atmosphere, much as Reich did. When the cones are placed below the knee or within two or three feet of the ground, dowsing tests indicate that the amount of energy emission is greatly lessened. Putting the cones in series amplifies the output. Unlike pyramid energy, the energy of a cone is not focused in the interior. The effect is as if the energy were spiralling around the outside toward the tip, where it focuses into a beam. My own experiments also show a substantial flow of energy from the base of the cone, whether the base is vertical or horizontal. This leads to some interesting speculation about wizard's caps, dunce caps and the conical hats worn by hard-working peasants in many parts of the world. At any rate, a conical cap is much more attractive on the head than a pyramid. Hyperbolas, used as antennas or solar ovens, are other cone variations.

If two cones, or a cone and a set of coils, are pointed head-on, the beams flatten out to form a circle of energy around each. In one experiment with the devices set forty feet apart, Cameron detected a sixty-foot circle of energy around each. But when one was beamed into the back of the other from behind, the output of the first was greatly increased. In fact, Cameron said that if one cone is beamed into another from any direction except head-on, it produces an amplifying effect. This is doubly interesting in view of a report I received indicating that a simple series of plastic hemispheres placed on edge and in line could dehydrate a fish.

Cameron also found by dowsing that a cone beam directed into the shoulder area of one's back would project straight out of the chest for a considerable distance. When amplified, such a beam supposedly produces a strong heat sensation on or in the part of the body it was directed toward. By projecting the cone beam at a mirror on a 45-degree angle, Cameron discovered that it was reflected at a 90-degree angle to the input, just like light. Recall that Mesmer, Reichenbach and Hieronymous also spoke of the reflecting qualities of the energy.

## Keely's Motor

In the latter half of the nineteenth century, around the time that Reichenbach was writing up his discoveries on the odic force, another man claimed to discover a new force in nature. Unlike Reichenbach, who was engaged in observation, this man was an inventor who even formed a company, called the Keely Motor Company, to exploit his discovery. Keely's motor supposedly worked by using principles of acoustics and the vibration patterns inherent in all materials. He claimed that he could break down water into hydrogen and oxygen without heat, cause an engine to run through the use of tuning forks, make metal spheres rise and fall in a tank of water by playing certain chords, completely disintegrate matter, and cause heavy objects to float through the air. A list of his inventions is intriguing: a transmitter wheel engine (the Keely motor), a globe engine, a globe generator, a compound disintegrator, a tubular resonator, a pocket-sized liberator, a vibratory accumulator, a vibraphone, a pneumatic rocket gun and a flying machine. Unfortunately, none of these are in existence today and no comprehensible plans are available. There are only a few frustrating drawings and incomplete reports.

For instance, a report in a newspaper of the time describes the Keely Motor as having a wheel of metal weighing seventy-two pounds and able to rotate freely on a stationary axis. The hub of the wheel is a cylinder containing resonant tubes parallel to the axis. There are eight spokes radiating outward, each with a "vitalized disc" at the end. A few inches from these discs is a stationary rim six inches wide and thirty-two inches in diameter. The inner wheel turns without touching this rim. On the inner surface of the rim are nine discs attached to resonating cylinders fixed to the outer surface. To this outer rim is attached a gold and silver wire which runs ten feet to a separate device (the generator) with a copper globe. Below the globe is a zither (a "sympathetic transmitter") which the operator strikes, modulating the tone with a knob. The force is transmitted to the globe, which converts it to the wire leading out from its center to the motor. Immediately, the inner wheel of the motor begins to turn rapidly.

In some fashion Keely is supposed to have caused sound-induced energy to travel along a wire to the resonating cylinders and through them to the nine vitalized discs, which "somehow" caused the inner wheel to move. It may be worth noting that at about this same time Reichenbach discovered that sound is one of the sources of *vril*, and also that this energy could be induced to travel along a wire.

Assuming Keely was working with *vril*, I can follow his procedure logically from the striking of the zither through the sympathetic vibrations of the copper ball and through the wire to the motor. Then I am lost, because I do not know the exact mechanisms by which the energy from the wire went from there through the resonating cylinders and into the "vitalized" discs. The latter, I suspect, were magnetized, as we know that *vril* is somehow associated with magnetism. It is not inconceivable that the sound-induced *vril* caused magnetic fields around the nine discs of the outer rim to become dynamic instead of static. This might exert a force upon the discs of the inner rim, putting the wheel into motion. This sounds like a reasonable explanation, but it is of no use until we learn how to make *vril* cause the magnetic fields to become dynamic.

A clue to the influence of magnetism is contained in another part of the above description. It says that the outer resonating cylinders were made of tubes and that "a requisite amount of the metallic volume" of the cylinder was obtained by enclosing some sewing needles within the tubes. "Curiously enough," it was said, "some of these needles at length become magnetic." Whether this was induced magnetism from the vitalized discs or caused by the incoming *vril* I cannot say. Reich mentioned that objects became magnetized under heavy concentrations of orgone. The fact that there were nine discs on the outer rim and eight on the inner wheel also suggests magnetism. A number of people in recent times have developed experimental motors based on offset magnets. Keely could have done the same, only using sound instead of electricity to start the motor. His wire led to the fixed rim and not the wheel; therefore some force had to enter and pass through the outer discs.

Keely's antigravity experiments were reportedly witnessed by several observers. In one experiment he is supposed to have caused an eight-pound model airplane to rise in the air and descend as gently as a feather. The plane was linked to a sympathetic transmitter by a silver and platinum wire. On another occasion he is said to have moved a five hundred horsepower engine from one end of his shop to the other, with the aid of a belt and other apparatus that he wore on his body. Keely felt that he was dealing with a latent energy existing in all matter (much like atomic energy) that could be liberated through the use of sound. This energy is supposed to manifest itself in three forms associated with gravity, magnetism and electricity. The three materials used in the wires, gold, silver and platinum, were supposed to be best, respectively, for transmitting the three forces. It is interesting to note that the Chinese use these three metals in acupuncture for providing the body with different types of energy from the atmosphere.

The linking of gravity with electromagnetism presents us with intriguing speculation. Actually, very little is known about gravity. It is almost completely ignored in modern technology, except for space travel and space medicine. It is utilized when convenient in such primitive ways as gravity-fed water lines, but that is like using a lodestone for a compass. We are familiar with the electromagnetic spectrum, but who is to say that there is not a magnetogravitic spectrum or an electrogravitic spectrum also? Perhaps this mysterious *vril*—which is not *quite* magnetism and not *quite* electricity, and which also has anomalous gravity effects—falls into one or both of those categories. After all, until we had the proper instruments we could not detect radio waves or gamma rays. Maybe we just have not yet designed the right instruments for *vril*.

Keely's description of how his antigravity device operated is no help. Here is a sample of his prose "explaining" how to liberate molecular energy:

*The second step is to liberate, according to symbolic meaning, the second harmonic bar on sixths, or neutralizing one, and the third, enharmonic ninths, which is the one counting from negative sevenths. Now all is in readiness for the transmissive nodal wire, one end of which must be attached to the magnetic dispersing ring, over the negative-sevenths cluster, and the other end to the high polar negative attractor.*

Only Keely could know what he meant by that.

We are left with the apparent fact that sound played a critical role in Keely's devices. Today sound, as sonic vibration, is used in a number of practical applications, such as to clean dishes, to remove tarnish, to operate a limited number of machines and for certain medical purposes. Reports dating back to Egyptian and other ancient cultures relate that the priesthood knew ways of using sound for levitation. It is a fact that one *feels* lighter when chanting certain mantras, especially when done in a strong *vril* field like the inside of a pyramid. In modern times in Europe, experiments were carried out with infrasound—which has too low a frequency to be heard—with terrifying results. A giant whistle was constructed, and the man who blew it fell to the ground, instantly dead. It is said that all his internal organs were turned to mush. In a much lighter vein, a researcher in the United States has claimed that certain frequency combinations can cause sexual excitement in women.

Sound, gravity and electromagnetism in relation to *vril* are an open field for further research.

### Electrophotography

A study of *vril* would not be complete without a look at electrophotography, more commonly known as Kirlian photography after one of its developers. Electrophotography is a means of taking pictures with a high-frequency electrical charge instead of light. In simple terms, the object to be photographed is placed on a piece of film laid on a capacitor setup. When high-frequency voltage is passed through the object, an image appears on the film.

The effects produced may change in detail according to such variables as type of equipment, frequency rates and humidity levels. In general one sees a highly luminescent outline of the object surrounded by a bright corona or halo, with flame-like flares issuing outward. In color photographs the corona is usually bluish-white, but all the colors of the rainbow can appear within the outline of the object itself. In leaves especially there are bubbles of color and clusters of light that produce very beautiful effects. To traditional scientists these effects are inexplicable. They should not be there. But the effects are too obvious to ignore, so a few feeble attempts at theory-making have been tried. One holds that it is simply corona discharge, similar to the effects produced around high-frequency electrical equipment or on pointed objects during electrical storms. By labeling the phenomenon with a familiar name, some scientists think they have solved the problem. But the fact is that corona discharge itself has not been thoroughly studied. Furthermore, the corona around the objects in electrophotography varies in ways that do not correspond to the common understanding of corona discharge around electrically charged objects. Another theory refers to such a corona as cold electron emission. This puts it in the same class as the famous St. Elmo's fire, a greenish ball of electrical energy that may form around a mast in a storm and frighten sailors. It is hard to say if this is correct since no one really understands what cold electron emission is. A Russian theory says that the field which is photographed is "biological plasma" or "bioplasma" as it is frequently called. Bioplasma is supposed to be an ensemble of excited electrons with a negative charge and other subatomic particles that reacts to magnetic and other fields.

Students of the occult traditions find no mystery in the phenomenon. In fact, they see it as a justification of what they have always claimed—that there is an aura of superphysical matter, invisible except to trained and

talented eyes, surrounding every object, living and
nonliving. Around living objects the color and quality
of this aura changes according to mood and environment. This tradition holds that energy from an individual can be transferred to another person or object
by means of this aura or field.

To the great consternation of many scientists, the
effects of the bioplasma or corona discharge recorded
on film correspond in a detailed way to the claims of
the occultists. For instance, many tests have been
carried out with so-called "psychic healers" to see if
they exchange anything with their patients. According
to photographs, the corona of the healer's forefinger
usually has a singular bright red emission during the
healing process, and the total size of the corona is
diminished after the healing. The corona of the patient's forefinger, on the other hand, increases in size
and brightness during the healing and stays that way
afterward. This is a definite indication that one is being
energized by the other. Attempts to get the same results
from nonhealers were not successful.

The "phantom leaf" effect is one that also disturbs
scientists and pleases occultists. Apparently, the
Kirlians of Russia were the first to discover this
through electrophotography, but it has been duplicated
in the United States. When 2 to 10 percent of the
matter in a leaf is cut away, there is still a "phantom"
corona where the missing section used to be. For the
occultists this proves the existence of the "astral body"
which interpenetrates the physical body but is not
caused by it. This effect also corresponds to the
phantom limb often experienced by amputees.
Scientists have no explanation of this acceptable to
them. The phantom limb effect is supposed to be
psychological. The phantom leaf effect is not even
supposed to be.

Further proof that what is photographed is not

merely the physical effect of high-frequency voltage going through an object is the fact that as a living object dies it ceases to emit light, regardless of the strength of the charge. This is most obvious with leaves, whose images fade and disappear after a few days. In one experiment an amputated human finger showed the same process: the "life energy" faded out with the onset of death. Significantly, this does not happen with metals. Though nonliving, they continue to emit light. This might be explained by the fact that metals usually act as electrical conductors and dead organic substances are usually insulators. Water dehydration may also be a factor in the organic changes. But the field changes in living matter go beyond such simplistic explanations. All of this is complicated by the fact that there is no general agreement on what the aura actually is.

Occultists and psychic healers have been bothered by the fact that hypnosis and an intake of alcohol both cause an increase in the size and brightness of the corona. However, if we consider that both of these tend to defocus the conscious mind and release inhibitory blocks, we can see it as the result of a more relaxed state. The Russians also found that many of the flare groupings recorded corresponded exactly with acupuncture points. Dramatic changes in the corona have been noted before and after treatment with acupuncture needles, depending on the points used. Furthermore, it has been demonstrated that field effects between people modify the size and brightness of the corona. In a series of experiments carried out by Thelma Moss and Kendall Johnson at U.C.L.A., it was found that the corona of male subjects varied greatly according to whether the photographer was male or female, whether a friend or a stranger, and whether friendly or aloof. Coronas of the fingers of two people on the same piece of film may appear to rebuff each other or blend together, depending on the relationship of the individuals.

Electrophotography offers many possibilities for testing theories and finding facts about *vril* transmission. For instance, tests could be made with a wide variety of crystals and *vril* generators, and the effects on individuals receiving energy from or imparting energy to them. Other tests might give clues for techniques of energizing inanimate objects and for improving healing methods. The greater the number of people participating in this research, the more we can expect to learn.

## Plasma

Plasma physics is a relatively new branch of science which will have a big impact on the study of *vril*. The ancients held there are four forms of matter: earth, water, air and fire (the Chinese said wood, water, air, fire and metal; and the Hawaiians said fire, water, wind and stone). Earth, of course, represented all solid substances, water all liquids, air all gases, and fire meant fire in all its forms. Early scientists accepted all of these except fire as forms of matter, until 1879. That is when Sir William Crookes found that a gas he had electrified in a tube became something other than a gas. He produced plasma, which he rightly concluded was a fourth state of matter, corresponding to the ancient label of fire.

The main difference between plasma and a gas is that plasma is affected by electromagnetic forces; plasma conducts electricity. We can see the use of plasma every day in neon tubes, for example, which are filled with glowing plasma. Another term for plasma, which may be more familiar to some, is ionized gas.

Ionization is a process by which an atom either loses an electron (making it a positive ion) or gains an extra electron (making it a negative ion). Here "positive" and "negative" refer to electrical charges. This condition permits the atoms thus modified to become subject to electromagnetic forces. Astronomy holds that the sun and all the stars are composed of plasma; the phenomenon of solar wind is a plasma wave; and the ionosphere and Van Allen belts surrounding the earth are made of plasma. On Earth, the most interesting use of plasma today may be in what is called a "magneto-hydro-dynamic" motor. While it holds the potential for pollution-free energy, the main problem is that at present the most efficient way to produce plasma is to heat a gas until the electrons break free and ionize it. Thus far standard fuels have to be used to do that, which of course add to pollution.

For many years in Europe and increasingly in the United States, plasma has been put to use for health. During certain seasons of the year in various parts of the world, hot, dry winds from the deserts blow over populated areas, causing excessive positive ionization of the atmosphere. Ordinarily the atmosphere has a rough balance of positive and negative ionization. But when the Santa Ana winds of California, the Harmattan winds of West Africa and the Feun winds of Europe are active, they produce clear skies, and, among stress-sensitive people, headaches, nausea, fatigue, irritability, arthritic and rheumatoid pain, and an increase in accidents. To offset this, negative ion generators were introduced, which tend to make one feel cool, refreshed, bright, alert and cheerful, even when positive ions are too abundant.

Now, what has this to do with *vril?* Just that the effects of both positive and negative ions are strikingly similar to *vril* effects from various sources. For many people positive ions are not debilitating but stimulating, as are *vril* sources such as pyramids and crystals. The same stress effects of excessive positive ionization can be noted under the high concentrations of *vril* found in certain orgone devices. On the other hand, the same beneficial effects of negative ions have been reported from many other kinds of *vril* devices, including human hands. It cannot be said at this point that *vril* is identical to ionized gas, but only that ionization produces effects like *vril* does, as do many other things.

## Theoretical Review

With many other examples left unmentioned, I bring this chapter to a close with a reminder that fruitful research must be based on a theoretical framework to give it cohesiveness, consistency and practicality. So far most researchers in this area have been groping in the dark, finding all kinds of effects, but without a theoretical framework to link them together. Until such a framework is established, we can only continue to grope, and whatever framework is finally decided upon must be comprehensible and usable by anyone with average intelligence. I do not believe that the universe was constructed to be understood only by Einsteins.

Many ancient systems of thought claim to have the theoretical framework already established, and it is possible that they do. But that does not help us a great deal right now. To thoroughly understand the Hindu framework, for example, and apply it, requires that one "become" a Hindu. It can be done, but I believe that the framework can and must be stated in terms we are already familiar with if we hope to make significant and immediate progress.

The theory that best fits my research holds that we are dealing with one energy, possibly polarized. This energy:

- induces subjective sensations of warmth, coolness, tingling, current flow or pressure, depending on the state of the perceiver;
- has subjective effects of physical well-being and mental clarity;
- has objective kinesthetic effects of inducing relaxation, which stimulates the healing process; of stimulating the function of all bodily processes; and in the presence of emotional resistance to physical change, of temporarily increasing pain and tension;
- has objective physical properties similar to but not identical with those of electromagnetism, gravity and light;
- is found in the presence of a multitude of diverse energetic and nonenergetic sources;
- is "psychoenergetic," that is, influences and is influenced by the mind.

I could hypothesize that we are dealing with a group of different energies that happen to have the same effect. But that would not be efficient if we want to focus on the practical effects and not the sources of the effects. If I want to stimulate a bodily function with *vril*, then I have a wide choice of means, such as hands, crystals, orgone accumulators, magnets, pyramids. But if my focus is on magnetism, for instance, then I am limited to the capabilities of magnets.

Another thing to note is that theories are used in two ways in science. On the one hand, they are used as a basis for testing the assumptions of the theory itself, with the intent to prove or disprove the theory. This follows the classical process known as the "scientific method." On the other hand, however, when a theory cannot easily be proven or disproven, it is used nevertheless as a guideline for research until a more effective theory comes along. For instance, the theories of the nature of electricity have not been proven or disproven, but they are used every day to provide electricity and electrical products. The assumption of gradualism in geology—the idea that earth changes take place slowly over a long period of time—is an unproven theory, yet it is a standard assumption used by geologists. And the theory of evolution, still unproven, forms the basis for a great deal of present-day scientific education and research. It is better to base actions on a reasonable guess than on no basis at all, especially if the guess yields practical results.

Today there is no way of knowing whether what I call *vril* is an actual energy. But by assuming that it is, we can produce very practical results.

# 11
# Future Prospects

The "state of the art" regarding *vril* research is approximately where the study of electricity was a century ago. There are major differences in today's conditions, however, that will modify the outcome considerably. An important one is the ease of communication. With television, radio, newspapers, magazines, books and a worldwide postal, telephone, fax and computer system, we can exchange information faster than ever before in history. The synergistic effect of this exchange makes air travel seem snail-like in comparison.

Another condition which will greatly assist the practical application of *vril* is the technology-oriented education system of the West. This means that many more people than ever before are acquainted with the basic principles on which technology is founded. Scientists are no longer a mysterious priesthood holding all the keys to knowledge. Laypersons will provide much of the vital research necessary to exploit this energy, perhaps even more than scientists. A real advantage for laypersons is that, while familiar with technological principles, they are not bound by traditional theories, which sometimes prevent scientists from breaking into new areas.

Now, also, there is new interest in ancient civilizations and in reinterpreting religious history and old legends in the light of modern findings, a field which might be called "neo-archeology." If the ancients could do such amazing things as moving huge stones, providing cold light and traveling through the air and possibly space by relatively simple means, there is no reason why we cannot do the same today.

Also affecting *vril* research in a positive way is the widespread and growing interest in psychic and paranormal phenomena. Factual data from these studies is proving beyond a reasonable doubt that there really are energies beyond or apart from those we are familiar with.

Finally, there is increasing dissatisfaction with the established ways of solving life's problems. Technology, medicine, psychology and many other modern systems, wondrous as some of their effects are, have not been able to heal, help or inspire on a large enough scale to suit the needs and desires of the world. And so more and more people are searching elsewhere for solutions.

The development and application of *vril* technology will not proceed without hindrance, however. Entrenched sectors of society with vested interests in current processes will oppose it all the way. For the full application of *vril* will upset the economy of the whole world, forcing huge shifts in emphasis and making tremendous amounts of equipment and many, many practices totally obsolete. It is essential to take this into account. Otherwise there is the possibility that *vril* research will be even more suppressed than in the past. The story has been repeated over and over again of people who have discovered applications of this energy and thought that the world would accept its benefits with open arms for the good of all mankind. But they found their process bought out and put in storage or themselves ridiculed and humiliated, perhaps even prosecuted or, worse, totally ignored. It would be foolish to pretend that that could not happen today.

Now let us look at some of the prospects for *vril* application and the possible effects resulting from those applications.

### Healing

Healing is risky in view of the fate of various researchers in this field, but the fact cannot be denied that *vril,* through several forms of application, does aid the healing process. However, in modern society drug medicine is a big business. The drug companies, of course, are interested in maintaining their large market, and the doctors who prescribe those drugs will be reluctant to abandon their years of drug-oriented training. Then there are the pharmacists, the bottlemakers, packagers, distributors and salespeople. *Vril* could obviate the need for most (not all) of that whole complex. Nevertheless, let's see what *could* happen if the application of *vril* to healing were widely accepted.

One application is already gaining ground. Acupuncture is based on balancing the *vril* (or *ch'i*) in the body by inserting thin needles at special points. It is taking hold in an increasing number of states and communities in the United States where colleges, degrees and licensing for this ancient Chinese art have been established. If the burgeoning trend toward alternative medicine continues, we can expect acupuncture and its derivatives like shiatsu (a form of "acupressure" in which finger pressure replaces needles) to become at least as popular within the next decade as chiropractic and homeopathy are now. Development of a theory of how those treatments work that is acceptable to mainstream thinking will speed this acceptance.

Electromagnetic treatment of disease is presently out-

lawed for the most part in the United States, but not
elsewhere. In Japan the use of magnets for healing is
quite open and popular, and magnets are even incorporated into jewelry and sandals with specific claims of
healing benefits. Especially as Japanese cultural and
economic influence increases, it is possible to foresee
electromagnetic treatment seriously considered in the
United States in coming years.

At one time I thought that devices like pyramids
would produce a revolution in healing practices
throughout the world. I have come to realize that, quite
aside from the resistance of vested interests, most
people are reluctant to keep up practices that are not
supported by their peers or authority figures, mainly
out of fear of ridicule. Even when people have experienced the effectiveness of such devices for relieving
pain, for example, I have known them to turn back to
aspirin because it is more "normal," though it might
not work as well. This is ironic as we still do not
understand how aspirin works. So, although pyramids,
cones, orgone devices and other *vril* generators might
effectively help the healing process, I do not predict
their widespread use in the near future. The use of
crystals for healing might proceed at a better rate, not
only because of their inherent beauty but because they
can be applied by practitioners who may develop the
aura of authority so important to healing.

Under names like "bioenergetics" and "therapeutic
touch," the transmission or movement of *vril* by human
hands for healing purposes is rapidly spreading, especially as thousands of people learn the techniques from
hundreds of teachers every year. With the right
approach this simple way to improve the health of
humans, animals and plants could spread like wildfire
across the world, thus greatly enhancing the standard
of living for Third World peoples, as well as for those

in developed countries. Its advantages are that it can be done in private, there are authorities in the medical profession who are beginning to use it, and, if done conservatively, it does not appear "weird."

You will notice that I have mentioned the word "authority" several times. This is because human healing is always highly influenced by belief systems. *Vril* may have healing benefits in itself, but its effects on humans is inhibited or enhanced by individual beliefs about health and healing, about techniques and processes, about tools and devices, and about the practitioners and authorities.

The acceptance of the use of *vril* in the healing field will go faster than traditionalists expect and slower than researchers would like, for reasons already mentioned. But one day *vril* generators may be standard equipment for use in postoperative convalescence and in the treatment of minor illnesses. We can expect an attempt to limit their medical use to treatment under a doctor's supervision, but that will probably fail as the authority of the medical profession continues to erode. Still, there probably will be, and ought to be, careful regulation to protect patients against exaggerated claims.

### Agriculture and Husbandry

The first attempts to use *vril* through psychotronic devices for destroying insects failed to gain a foothold in the United States because of the opposition of the producers of insecticides, aided by the government. The attempt will be made again, probably in other countries, and the process will probably reenter the United States because of successes made known by word of mouth. The process in the U.S. is not dead; it is operating on a small scale and ready to leap into action again when the time is right. While big farmers using the process might mean more money for the operators, it is more likely that a restart will be made among small farmers and gardeners. Then, when there is enough documented evidence of its effectiveness in a multitude of small operations, it will move back into the big-time. The right time will be when larger-scale farmers hear enough about it to begin asking for it.

*Vril* can be used both to speed up the growth of plants and to provide more abundant crops. Fertilizer interests will be upset when acceptance of this starts on a large scale. *Vril* can be used to treat seeds before they are planted. Certain types of *vril* may be installed in the fields themselves, possibly spreading the *vril* by means of ground wires. Research will be needed to determine the proper dosage based on the age and type of plant. More likely, the easier process of treating the water before it reaches the fields will gain acceptance first. There are already devices in preparation, using Reichian principles, that treat water as it flows through a pipe. Patrick Flanagan, an inventor and energy researcher, used a device consisting of water flowing through a coil inside a pyramid, but other configurations dispense with the pyramid entirely. Manufacturers would probably make lease arrangements with large-scale users, but a huge market could be available through home garden supply chains using small, simple treatment devices. Flower growers and retailers may furnish another large market for *vril* generators, both for producing more and healthier flowers and for keeping the flowers fresher longer in the shops.

Beside the direct treatment of soil, water and plants, harvested grain can also be treated. *Vril* has a dehydrating effect and a bacteria-retardating effect. We may see special generators used in grain storage silos to cut losses from mildew and rot and permit grain to be stored longer without the use of dangerous chemicals. It may also be possible to produce dehydrated foods similar to freeze-dried at a much cheaper cost.

Tremendous possibilities open up with the application of *vril* to the treatment of animals. Mice with skin wounds on their backs were treated in oracs and showed remarkable speed in healing as compared to controls. Restrictions required for healing humans does not apply to animals, an advantage for research. The chicken industry puts up with large losses, and *vril* might reduce those losses to a very profitable degree. Treatment of all animals could result in higher quality and more abundant food supplies. The pet market is not to be overlooked, either. Successful healing of animals with *vril* might help pave the way for greater acceptance of such treatments for humans.

## Pollution

According to Czech research, psychotronic generators can precipitate nonprecipitable solutions, and according to my own research, bacterial pollutants can be eliminated from water with certain *vril* generators. Under some conditions algae growth can be retarded, too. Further research may lead to the real possibility of cleaning up our streams, lakes and rivers, not to speak of our swimming pools. Another possibility, though basic research is lacking, is to place *vril* generators in smokestacks or car exhausts to precipitate out the polluting chemicals.

Most important of all is the production of pollution-free motors operating from *vril* generators, which cut down on noise pollution as well. Probably one of the greatest potentials for this is in converting *vril* to electricity, as Reich apparently did and as my battery experiment indicated may be possible. A variation of the Keely Motor may accomplish this if someone finds the proper key to build it.

The implication of *vril* motors may be frightening to many people. It could totally eliminate the need for fuels such as coal, gas and oil, except for special applications. This would mean restructuring in the fuel-producing countries and in the major oil companies and relocating the millions of people who work for and service them. The person who first invents a workable and efficient *vril* motor, rather than having the world beat a path to his door, will be lucky if his house is not boarded up with him inside. But, like many developments in the past, I believe the breakthrough will come from several people at once and in different parts of the world. The procedure will probably be so simple that it will spread too fast to be stopped. Countries which are totally dependent on outside fuel supplies will be most interested, but political and extended economic interests may make for a difficult introduction even for them.

Not only fuel interests but utility companies risk losing business with the introduction of *vril* motors. It may become possible for people to meet their electricity needs with home generators that are noise-free and practically costless. It would be beautiful to have the cities and countryside free of power lines, but they will not come down easily. Still, change is inevitable, and all this is going to happen. However, at present it looks as if the great breakthrough in cheap and abundant electricity may come through more efficient and less expensive solar cells, but not necessarily.

### Transportation

With efficient and inexpensive *vril* motors available, the combustion engine will have had its day, though it will not give up without a fight. Automobile manufacturers, like oil companies, are too big to lie down quietly without trying to protect their interests. Since somebody has to make the motors and put them in the cars, the big companies may either refuse to do it or monopolize the process so as to keep profits high. Even so, it would help the exhaust pollution problem. But it is possible that *vril* motors will be introduced first in small vehicles like motor scooters and motorcycles and in public transportation.

*Vril* motors mean quiet, electrical driving with no fuel stops, charging stops or heavy batteries. A whole way of highway life would have to change. For psychological purposes artificial engine noise would probably have to be incorporated into the new motors, but it need not be as loud as what we have now. With no limits on fuel, there may have to be limits on the numbers of vehicles allowed. However, mass transport systems would be much more feasible economically and would undoubtedly grow in importance.

Air travel would undergo major modifications with the use of *vril* engines capable of lifting heavy loads. With no need for massive fuel loads, planes could carry more passengers and cargo. Double and triple decker planes might become more feasible. If the levitation effects of *vril* can be duplicated and made economically interesting, the changes would be truly revolutionary. After all, efficient solar-powered engines with lightweight batteries or safe fusion motors could work as well as *vril* motors in ordinary circumstances. But a levitation motor would allow for smaller airports in more locations and much larger planes. And the potential effect on space travel is obvious. Of course, this could be a long way in the future.

## Construction

If the levitation effect could be harnessed, the construction industry might be one of the first to take advantage of it. Heavy duty cranes and complicated supports would no longer be necessary. Unwieldy building components and things like prefabricated bridges could be towed through the air to their sites. Whole communities could be constructed at a factory and set in place on prepared foundations. Architecture would be revolutionized as well, with airy structures or gigantic ones made possible in places where they could not have been before.

## War

The military potential of all aspects of *vril* utilization is significant and can be frightening. *Vril* motors would reduce many costs for military equipment and logistics in any number of ways. Already, nuclear engines are allowing aircraft carriers and submarines to go without refueling for a decade or more. Strategy and tactics would change dramatically if fuel were no longer a consideration for trucks and tanks and missiles. And the military possibilities introduced by levitation boggle the mind. So cheap and abundant energy will be a boon to humankind only if we continue to teach and promote the ways and benefits of peace.

## Summary

In this book I have taken you through an introduction to some of the research that has been done and is being done in what I have called *vril* physics. Mesmer's deep insights into the nature of *vril;* Reichenbach's demonstration of the place of human sensory capabilities in research; Reich's far-reaching investigation in the field of orgonomy; the importance of shape and the ease of generating pyramid energy; the vital role of the mind in directing and controlling energy in radionics and psychotronics; research in the little known field of vivaxis;

research ideas and activities that generate extra energy—all these rather recent discoveries and developments are merely beginning to recover a technology known long ago in ancient cultures.

But the overall purpose behind this whole presentation is not merely to add to your store of knowledge. It is to give you enough keys, hints and inside information to stir you into active research of your own, if you have not already begun, and into more productive research if you have.

I close by expressing my sincere hope that you will profit from what you have read, and that you will share that profit with others. Knowledge shared leads to wisdom; knowledge unshared leads to tyranny. It is fitting to end with the ancient cry of Hawaiian kahuna priests from the oracle tower of their temples:

LET THAT WHICH IS UNKNOWN BECOME KNOWN.

# Appendix:
# Experimental Procedures

*This appendix consists of the third chapter of my book,* Pyramid Energy Handbook *entitled "How To Set Up Experiments" (Warner, 1977), which is relevant to experimenting with* vril. *Although the information is oriented toward experiments with pyramids, the procedure described can be applied to any kind of* vril *research.*

From listening to people's responses when you tell them some of the unusual things that even a cardboard pyramid is supposed to do, you think that we are a society without any will power or discernment. It gets worse when you get them to try something like the taste test. The most common reaction I receive from people confronted with pyramid energy for the first time is, "Well, that's just suggestion!" What they are saying is that by merely mentioning the possibility that they would taste a difference with pyramid-treated water I caused them to experience it. Wow! I wish I really had that much power. But apparently I don't because when I then suggest that they finance some research I only get a blank stare.

It is both amazing and ironic to realize how many people have been programmed to believe that they are easily suggestible (when experience conflicts with "logic") and that so much of reality is a function of belief. For many people think that the pyramid works if you believe in it. This can be rather disheartening for the novice researcher who is eager to share his or her knowledge with others. On the other hand, there are wild claims made by certain so-called researchers that discredit the whole field of pyramid energy because they are so easily refuted by simple experiments. In those cases, desire, or belief, does overcome reality— for the claimants, at least.

To help ease your own mind about the energy, to aid you in overcoming the healthy skepticism of friends and relatives, and to assist you in determining what pyramids can and cannot do, I am going to use the question-and-answer format to explain how to set up experiments in a scientific manner. This will give your findings more credibility, even though the National Academy of Science may not accept your results as proof of anything. The point is that by using an organized method in your research you will eliminate much of the erroneous reporting that is due to over-enthusiasm or carelessness.

*Okay, what's the first thing to do?*

Get a pyramid. That isn't as facetious as it sounds, honest. Before you begin, you must have in mind the kind of experiment you want to perform. Remember, you have your choice among pyramids of different shapes, materials, and construction (framework as opposed to solid sides, for example). Probably, though, you will want to begin with something small and simple. For beginning research I would recommend a cardboard pyramid 6 inches high. You can do an awful lot with that before your interest takes you into fancier, larger, and/or more expensive models.

*Then what?*

Get a notebook. A spiral-bound notebook with 8½" by

11″ pages is a good choice, but you might prefer a loose leaf so you can take out pages and photocopy them. This book will contain your research results. The better organized it is, the easier it will be for you to duplicate, modify, and refer back to your experiments.

At the top of the first page, put the date and the number of your first experiment. It is a good idea to number all your experiments. The easiest way being to start with "1" and head toward infinity. But if you think you will be experimenting with several kinds of pyramids, you might want to establish a simple kind of code to make reference easier. For instance, experiments with your 6-inch cardboard pyramid could be numbered CP6/1, CP6/2, CP6/3, etc. and those with a 12-inch high aluminum frame, AF12/1, AF12/2, AF12/3, and so on.

Next, write down the word "Objective," and after it put down the reason you are conducting this experiment. Perhaps it is to see whether the pyramid can really sharpen your razor blades or preserve fruit. Or you might be testing for the effects of turning the pyramid away from magnetic north. Whatever it is, state it clearly in this section so that you don't forget what it is you are trying to find out.

Title the following section "Materials," and list here everything you are using for the experiment, being as specific as possible. A typical list might be "one 6-inch cardboard Cheops model pyramid; one Gillette blue blade; one plastic 3-inch stand." You will also want to list any materials you are using for comparison, such as a second blade. If you are testing liquids for taste, list the source (tap water, Yuban, Johnnie Walker) and make a notation of the temperature. For most purposes a simple hot, warm, cool or cold will do. This is important because temperature does affect taste.

The next section should be titled "Procedure." This is where you will describe how you are going to carry out the experiment. As an example, you could say that after shaving you are going to place a razor blade inside the pyramid on top of the stand with the long axis north and south, that you are going to leave it there for 24 hours before testing on your beard again, and that you are going to keep up this experiment for a period of 3 weeks. It is very important that this section be well detailed, because here is where you can get ideas for modifying future experiments and perhaps find out what you did wrong if the experiment didn't seem to work.

I would suggest another section, either before or after the previous one, titled "Environment." Pyramids are well known to be cantankerous. Sometimes they don't work even when you think you've done everything right. Karl Drbal wrote that the "last twenty-five years have [been] for me a long experimental sequence, with each shaving itself an experimental experience which has sometimes informed me, by unexpected changes in the sharpness of the blade, of some meteorological or cosmic disturbance . . . often after a day when I received a poor shave I was surprised the next day by receiving, from the same blade, an excellent shave." This experience is duplicated in my early research notes before I was aware of the details of Drbal's work. So, under "Environment" note weather conditions, time of day, and, if you can, the position of the moon and whether sunspots are active. In addition, make a note of where the experiment is being conducted, on what kind of surface, and whether it is close to electrical devices. There is a lot of controversy about the effect of electrical devices on pyramids. Maybe your research will help establish some facts. [N.B. since *vril* is psychoenergetic, note any strong emotional states that may occur near the pyramid during the period of the experiment.]

"Results" is the title of the next section. Now you have a place to record what happens during your experiment. Make this part as objective as possible. Just note results as they appear to you. Make no judgments and draw no conclusions, as yet. If your experiment is ongoing, note the results by date and/or time.

Finally, you may have a section called "Conclusions." These are your conclusions based on the results of your experiment. You might decide that "the pyramid really does sharpen blades," or "the taste test was inconclusive, will have to try at a different temperature next time." In other words, it is a summary of your ideas, thoughts, criticisms and recommendations about the experiment. This section will become a rich source of future experimental ideas.

There is no telling how much space each experimental write-up will take. It depends a lot on how much detail you like to put down, and how involved or time-consuming the experiment is. In some cases my notebook has three experiments on a single page, while in others one experiment may take five pages or more. Two factors which play a role in determining how complicated an experiment is going to be are "controls" and "variables."

*What is a control, since you obviously want the question?*

Thank you. A control is something like a second experiment that goes on at the same time as another, only the conditions are changed. For example, let's say you are testing the possible change of taste in a glass of tap water after placing it under a pyramid for 5 minutes. You can taste the water first and then taste it after it has been under the pyramid, but there is the chance that you will have forgotten how it tasted in the first place. So a better way is to use a control, that is, a

second glass of water drawn at the same time as the
first test glass and using the same kind of container.
Now, after the 5 minutes are over, you can taste the
"control" glass, the one left out under ordinary conditions, and compare it to the "test" glass, the one
left under the pyramid. You see, the control is the
experiment in which everything is the same *except* the
thing you are testing for. This helps you decide
whether the thing being tested is having any effect.
In testing a pyramid, another pyramid could be the
control if it were disoriented by 45 degrees. That would
tell you if magnetic north were having the effect it is
supposed to. In using controls you have to be careful
not to introduce any factors that make the experiment
invalid. A glass of ice water should not be used as a
control for a test glass of freshly drawn tap water, for
instance. An aluminum pyramid should not be tested
against a cardboard one if what you are testing for is
the effect of magnetic north and not the effect of the
different materials. The control has to be as nearly
identical to the test object as possible for a controlled
experiment to have any meaning. And controlled experiments are much more highly regarded than uncon-
trolled experiments. In some cases a control experiment can be run at a different time than the test. You
can test a blue blade to see how many shaves you can
get from it, and then test a blue blade which has been
under a pyramid between shaves for comparison. Then
your only variables are outside forces that might
change from day to day.

*Now, may I ask, what are variables?*
   Experimentally speaking, a variable is anything which
changes, or which is changed. It is the opposite of a
"constant," that which does not change. Temperature
would be a variable if your control glass of water is put

outside in the winter while your test glass is put under the pyramid next to a heater. That means that the effect of temperature is another thing that would have to be taken into consideration when evaluating the results of your experiment. If your glasses are identical, the glass would be a constant, a factor that would not have to be taken into consideration until you tried another type of glass, when it would become a variable. If you use blue blades in an experiment, the type of blade is a constant, but if you use a blue blade for the test and a stainless steel for the control, the type of blade is a variable. This means that a scientist could say that the results may have more to do with the difference in the type of blade used than in the fact that a pyramid was used to cover one. The essence of a good controlled experiment is reducing the variables to a minimum. This isn't easy to do in home experiments. If your wife, husband, child or pet knocks one part of your experiment askew midway through, that becomes a variable that has to be taken into account when reaching your conclusions.

Variables get to be a real pain when testing pyramid effects on humans because humans are so variable within themselves and between each other. A man's beard grows at different rates during a month, and diet can affect the oiliness of his skin, which would affect the pull of the blade, and these become variables which have to be considered. The tasting ability of people varies widely, especially between smokers and non-smokers, and this certainly affects any conclusions you might draw from the reactions of people to a taste test.

There are two ways to help overcome this difficulty. One is to extend the time of the experiment so that variables tend to cancel themselves out. Running a razor blade experiment for two weeks is not as valid as running one for four months. It is not uncommon for a person to get 120 shaves from a blue blade kept under a pyramid, but try to get the same, or anywhere near the same, without the pyramid. True, one person, because of the nature of his skin, and beard, might only get 50 shaves, another only 90, but compared to the usual 7 to 10, this is highly significant.

Another way to reduce the importance of variables is to multiply the number of test subjects. Trying the taste test on two people is not very convincing, but when twenty-five, fifty or a hundred people try the test and 75 percent of them report a difference in taste, then you can be more sure of your results.

*I have heard of a blind test. What is that?*

A blind test is one in which the subject, a person used in an experiment, doesn't know which is the test and which is the control. If you are testing for taste and you want to run a blind test, you will put the subject in another room (or blindfold him) and bring him the control glass and the test glass without letting him know which is which. That makes his reaction more valid because he doesn't have any subconscious preconceptions about how he is supposed to react.

*Is a double-blind test the same thing?*

No, a double-blind test is intended to eliminate the possibility that the experimenter might be giving the subject some unconscious clues, like holding one glass a little forward of the other or looking expectant when he tries the test glass. The scientists who devised this were afraid that the subject would try to please the experimenter even without consciously wanting to. So in this case, the person carrying out the experiment with the subject doesn't even know which is the test and which is the control. He uses someone else to carry out his experiment. At home you could do this with three rooms. In one you would have your pyramid with the water under it and the control glass. Then you would take both glasses into the second room and leave them there while you return to the first room. Of course, you would have marked them in some way so only you would know which was which. Then your Aunt Agatha would come into the second room and carry them out to your Uncle Wolfgang (the subject) in the third room, where he would taste them. Aunt Agatha would note his reactions and then call you out so you could delightedly say, "See, I told you!" Or, be disappointed and try again.

*Is there any other reason for experimenting besides proving something to myself?*

Yes! You will not merely be repeating what others have done, exciting as that can be. The field of pyramid energy is so new that it is wide open to new ideas and new kinds of tests. Just by working at home you could discover something that everyone else has overlooked. As this is being written, the news has come out that an amateur astronomer in Japan with a small telescope has discovered a new comet missed by all the hundreds of professional astronomers around the world using the best and most refined equipment. And people have been scanning the skies for centuries. Nearly every month I receive a letter from someone who has found out something new about pyramids, and every week people give me new ideas about experiments that I haven't the time to follow up. The knowledge is there, and the more people we have working with pyramids, the sooner we will know more about them and be able to apply that knowledge more effectively. Even mistakes can lead to new information and new uses.

*What about people who refuse to believe you even after your experiments show it works?*

Your experimental work will give you more confidence in discussing pyramid energy with people, but don't waste your time trying to break down unbreakable barriers. You will meet four kinds of people when the subject comes up, not including those who have experimented with it like you. First are those who will believe about anything you say without checking. They are a bore. Then there are the healthy skeptics, who are the best of the lot. The nineteenth century science they were taught in school (and it is still being taught) doesn't prepare them for the fact that a piece of cardboard can exhibit properties not usually associated with cardboard but they are still willing to be shown whether or not it is true. They will question you sharply, and you had better know your subject and be honest about not knowing what you don't know. However, if they experience the effects of the energy, they won't be afraid to acknowledge it. Next are the brickheads. Anything that goes outside of the bounds of what they already know is false, stupid and probably dangerous. They can set your teeth on edge and had best be avoided. The worst of the four are the pseudo-intellectuals. They will undermine your confidence by quoting a dozen theories either stating that pyramids can't work or that the effects are due to something other than pyramids. They won't experiment, however, because that might upset their theories.

Do your experiments, draw your own conclusions, compare them with what others say or have written, and then, while the devout believers are just oohing and aahing, the brickheads are running away, and the pseudo-intellectuals are looking smug, go out and *use* the stuff for your own benefit.

# Bibliography

## Chapter 1—Clues from the Ancients

Berlitz, Charles. *Mysteries From Forgotten Worlds.* Dell Publishing Co. New York, 1972.

Cayce, Edgar Evans. *Edgar Cayce On Atlantis.* Warner Paperback Library. New York, 1972.

Charroux, Robert. *One Hundred Thousand Years of Man's Unknown History.* Berkley Medallion Books. New York, 1971.

____. *The Gods Unknown.* Berkley Medallion Books. New York, 1974.

Donnelly, Ignatius. *Atlantis: The Antediluvian World.* Gramercy Publishing Co. New York, 1949.

Drake, W. Raymond. *Gods and Spacemen in the Ancient East.* Signet Books. New York, 1973.

____. *Gods and Spacemen in the Ancient West.* Signet Books. New York, 1974.

Kolosimo, Peter. *Not of This World.* Bantam Books. New York, 1973.

Long, Max Freedom. *The Secret Science Behind Miracles.* De Vorss & Co. Los Angeles, 1954.

Mann, Felix. *Acupuncture.* Vintage Books. New York, 1972.

Michell, John. *The View Over Atlantis.* Ballantine Books. New York, 1972.

Pauwels, Louis and Jacques Bergier. *The Eternal Man.* Avon Books. New York, 1973.

Sendy, Jean. *The Coming of the Gods.* Berkley Medallion Books. New York, 1973.

_____. *Those Gods Who Made Heaven and Earth.* Berkley Medallion Books. New York, 1972.

Tomas, Andrew. *We Are Not the First.* Bantam Books. New York, 1973.

_____. *The Home of the Gods.* Berkley Medallion Books. New York, 1974.

Trench, Brinslev Le Poer. *Temple of the Stars.* Ballantine Books. New York, 1974.

Von Daniken, Erich. *Chariots of the Gods?* Bantam Books. New York, 1972.

_____. *Gods From Outer Space.* Bantam Books. New York, 1972.

White, John, and Stanley Krippner, editors. *Future Science.* Anchor Books. New York, 1977.

## Chapter 2—The Vril of Mesmer

Barth, George. *The Mesmerist's Manual of Phenomena and Practice.* H. Balliere. London, 1851.

Goldsmith, Margaret. *A History of Mesmerism.* Doubleday, Doran & Co. New York, 1934.

## Chapter 3—The Odic Force and Reichenbach

Von Reichenbach, Charles. *The Od Force.* Health Research (reprint of 1854 edition). Mokelumne Hill, CA, 1965.

_____. *Physico-Physiological Researches on the Dynamics of Magnetism, Electricity, Heat, Light, Crystallization, and Chemism, in Their Relations to Vital Force.* Health Research (reprint of 1851 edition). Mokelumne Hill, CA, 1965.

## Chapter 4—Wilhelm Reich and Orgone Energy

Mann, W. Edward. *Orgone, Reich and Eros.* Touchstone Books. New York, 1973.

"The Orgone Energy Accumulator." The Wilhelm
   Reich Foundation. Rangeley, Maine, 1951.
Reich, Wilhelm. *Selected Writings.* Noonday Press.
   New York, 1971.
\_\_\_\_. *The Cancer Biopathy.* Farrar, Strauss & Giroux.
   New York, 1973.

**Chapter 5—The Power Behind Pyramidology**
Cox, Bill and Georgiana Teeple, editors. *The Pyramid
   Guide.* El Cariso Publications, Elsinore, CA.
Flanagan, G. Pat. *Pyramid Power.* Pyramid Publishers.
   Glendale, CA, 1973.
King, Serge. *Pyramid Energy Handbook.* Warner Books.
   New York, 1977.
Ostrander, Sheila, and Lynn Schroeder. *Psychic Discoveries Behind the Iron Curtain.* Bantam Books. New
   York, 1971.
Smith, Warren. "Mysterious Pyramids Around The
   World." *Saga Magazine.* October, 1973.
Tompkins, Peter. *Secrets of the Great Pyramid.* Harper
   & Row. New York, 1971.

**Chapter 6—Radionics: Detecting Subtle
Radiation?**
Cameron, Verne L. *Aquavideo.* El Cariso Publications.
   Elsinore, CA, 1970.
Long, Max Freedom. *Psychometric Analysis.* De Vorss
   & Co. Santa Monica, 1959.
Tompkins, Peter and Christopher Bird. *The Secret Life
   of Plants.* Harper & Row. New York, 1973.

**Chapter 7—Psychotronics: Transmission
at a Distance**
Abrams, Albert. "The Electronic Reactions of Abrams."
   Health Research (reprint of 1922 article). Mokelumne
   Hill, CA, 1972.
King, Serge. "Explorations In Paraphysics." *Beyond
   Reality.* July/August, 1974.

Layne, Mead, editor. *The Cameron Aurameter.* Borderland Sciences Research Foundation. Vista, CA, 1972.

Ostrander & Schroeder. *Psychic Discoveries.*

Watson, Lyall. *Supernature.* Anchor Press. New York, 1973.

## Chapter 8—Vivaxis: Attuning to the Earth's Energies

Nixon, Frances. *Born To Be Magnetic. Volume I.* Magnetic Publishers. Victoria, B.C., 1971.

____. *Born To Be Magnetic, Volume II.* Magnetic Publishers. Victoria, B.C., 1973.

## Chapter 9—Geomancy: Harmonizing Yin and Yang

King, Serge. "Aloha Process Training: The Shaman Discoverer Course." Kauai, Hawaii, 1991.

Walters, Derek. *Feng Shui: The Chinese Art of Designing a Harmonious Environment.* Simon & Schuster. New York, 1988.

Waters, Frank. *Book of the Hopi.* Ballantine Books, New York, 1974.

## Chapter 10—Extra Energy

Bova, Ben. *The Fourth State of Matter.* Mentor Books. New York, 1974.

Krippner, Stanley and Daniel Rubin, editors. *The Kirlian Aura.* Anchor Books. New York, 1974.

Layne, Mead. *The Cameron Aurameter.*

Sykes, Egerton. *The Keely Mystery.* Markham House Press, Ltd. London, 1964.

# Index

QUEST BOOKS
are published by
The Theosophical Society in America,
Wheaton, Illinois 60189-0270,
a branch of a world organization
dedicated to the promotion of the unity of
humanity and the encouragement of the study of
religion, philosophy, and science, to the end that
we may better understand ourselves and our place in
the universe. The Society stands for complete
freedom of individual search and belief.
In the Classics Series well-known
theosophical works are made
available in popular editions.

There are over 250 Quest books now
in print. These include books on

Meditation
Yoga
Reincarnation
Psychology
Theosophy
Astrology
Healing
Religion
ESP

For a free catalog, write to:

**QUEST BOOKS**
**306 West Geneva Road**
**Wheaton, Illinois 60187**

# THE POWER OF PLACE

James A. Swan, Ph.D.

**Stonehenge . . . the Himalayas . . . the sacred river Ganges . . . the Great Pyramid of Giza . . . these places affect us profoundly.** But until now, few have explored why such places are revered. In this provocative work, James Swan has collected essays on sacred places and their effect on human beings. **In an age when you may feel you have lost your connection to the planet, this book will help you discover your own relationship to the life around you.**

> *"Jim Swan continues his expert efforts to educate us about our relationship to the earth."*
> —Marilyn Christiano, Editor, *Voice of America*

> *". . . it's exciting, beautifully produced, highly intelligent, and fun. A superior work."*
> —Joseph Terrano, *Friend's Review*

> *"Jim Swan should be commended for creating a multi-cultural overview of the role of sacred places in all people's lives."*
> —Zoh M. Hieronimus, 21st Century Radio's Hieronimus & Co.

> *"This book is an important step on the path of creating a modern "Land Ethic" that cherishes humanity, other living creatures, and the land that sustains all life."*
> —Evelyn Martin, former director with the American Planning Assn.

> *"A superior anthology of articles. An intelligent, lucid excursion into the power of heart and mind, soul and place."*
> — *The Book Reader*

**Jim Swan** is currently Associate Professor of Anthropology at the California Institute of Integral Studies and with his wife Roberta is co-producer of Spirit of Place symposia series. He was one of the founding members of the Division of Environment and Population Psychology at the American Psychological Association. Swan has published over 100 articles in magzines such as *Shaman's Drum, Audubon,* and *Environmental Health Digest.*

# NATIVE HEALER

## Medicine Grizzlybear Lake

Many claim to be healers and spiritual teachers; the author is both. Here he explains how a person is called to be a medicine man or woman and the trials and tests of a candidate. Lake gives an exciting glimpse into the world of Native American shamanism. He was trained by numerous Native American teachers, including Rolling Thunder, and has conducted hundreds of ceremonies and lectures.

*"... very interesting account of a native American Indian healer's apprenticeship and practice..."*

— Serge Kahili King
author of *Imagineering for Health* and *Earth Energies*

*"... wonderful reading and full of important psychological, anthropological and spiritual information."*

— James A. Swan, Ph.D., author of *The Power of Place*

*"... it is a joy for me to read this work of Medicine Grizzlybear..."*

— Brooke Medicine Eagle

*"... a rare opportunity... to learn about shamanism from somebody who has been taught, trained, studied, and practiced in both worlds and societies. I therefore highy recommend it..."*

— Rolling Thunder, Inter-tribal Medicine Man

*"I highly recommend his book to all those who are feeling the expansion of spiritual awareness in their hearts and those who wish to understand the direct tradition of shamanism whose course is the same throughout many nations of indigenous people."*

— Dhyani Ywahoo, Spiritual Director, Sunray Meditation Society

*"In* Native Healer *we are reminded that healing is a powerful culturally endorsed ritual whose practitioners use skills and wisdom accumulated for centuries to help patients garner their most powerful self-healing responses."*

— Carl A. Hammerschlag, M.D., author of *The Dancing Healers*